"When Sandra and Michael left London to live in Hong Kong they were following a life path that was swept without warning from under their feet when Michael was found to have a tumour in his heart. Their daughter, Diana, was ten months old. What follows is a moving and courageous story of a young family engaging with extraordinary situations in a way that reminds us all of the precious value of life, community and friendships. In facing the reality of living with dying in an open and honest way they both show us what it means to end something and how to have faith in the formation of something new. This book delivers the message that life does not have to become a threat when painful things happen and that we can grow from what life presents us."

— Terry Cooper and Jenner Roth,
Founder Directors, Spectrum, London, UK

"Sandra Keys shows how it is possible to navigate a process of transformational change in a way that reconstructs meaning both in her own life and that of others. To do so with candor in the face of unrelenting loss is an act of courage; to do so with inspiration, with the deft hand of an inveterate storyteller, and even with irony and humor is an act of artistry."

— Dr. Robert A. Neimeyer,
author of *Lessons of Loss: A Guide to Coping*;
Professor and Director of Psychotherapy Research,
Department of Psychology, University of Memphis

Commentary from the medical experts on

Where Would You Like Your Dishwasher?

"This is an endearing story of a family coping with the life-threatening illness of a husband, a father, and of the difficult choices they were faced with. Michael Keys' simple wish to lead a life without frailty given the uncertainties of any medical cure for his condition inspired us to think in dimensions beyond the boundaries of clinical medicine. His legacy lives on in the body of knowledge that he selflessly enabled us to acquire in the course of our engagement with his rare tumor."

— Dr. Shekhar Madhukar Kumta,
MBBS, Master of Surgery (Ortho), Ph.D, Assistant Dean (Education),
Department of Orthopaedics & Traumatology,
Faculty of Medicine, The Chinese University of Hong Kong

"Michael Keys' life experience with illness is about hope, optimism and determination. Our faith is in the hand of God, and I learned from Michael that I should never give up in helping any patient."

— Dr. Ahmed A. Arifi,
MD, FRCS (UK), FCSHK
Consultant Cardiac Surgeon-Director of Clinical Research,
King Abdulaziz Cardiac Centre, Riyadh, Saudi Arabia

Where Would You Like Your Dishwasher?

My Story of Life, Love and Loss

SANDRA KEYS

For Lynda,

With love, Sandra L x

HAVEN
BOOKS

Where Would You Like Your Dishwasher?

Published in Hong Kong by Haven Books
www.havenbooksonline.com

ISBN 978-988-18967-1-1

Cover design by Candace Campos
Layout design by Katie Kwan
Editing by Charles Neal, Jilly Mangles and Michelle Low

DISCLAIMERS
This book is written with the recollection and memory of the author in relation to the events and information about the persons named. While every effort has been taken to ensure total accuracy and objectivity, the author and the publisher are not to be held liable for any errors that may have been made. Readers are advised that information provided in relation to events and persons named in this book may therefore be inaccurate and therefore they should not rely solely on such information.

Every effort is taken to credit original authors and to respect copyright for all the quotations that are shown in this book, the goal of which is to help other people who face similar difficult situations to those experienced by the author. If anyone has any concerns that copyright is not fully respected, then we would be very grateful if you could please let us know immediately so that we can rectify this situation. Thank you for your understanding on the personal and sensitive nature of the topic and aim of this book.

For Diana,

in memory of Michael.

With all my love, Mum x

Our heartfelt thanks are given to the Prince of Wales Hospital in Shatin, Hong Kong. The world class medical care provided by the hospital literally extended Michael's life by eight years instead of the anticipated six months following diagnosis of cardiac leiomyosarcoma. Particular thanks are given to Dr. Choi and Dr. Kwan from the Oncology team, to Dr. Arifi, Cardiac Surgeon and to Dr. Kumta, Orthopedic Surgeon. Special mention is also given to all the staff especially the team on the private ward and the physiotherapy team who offered constant care and support way above and beyond the call of duty. Remarkably this government teaching hospital came to feel like home to us over the years. This is no small achievement and words cannot easily express the depth of our family's gratitude.

Sandra Keys

Table of Contents

Foreword

As an advocate for hospice and palliative care in Hong Kong, I received a call from an expatriate lady seeking information on English-speaking home care support for a dying patient. Mrs Sandra Keys wanted to find out if it would be possible to take her husband, Michael, home to spend his last days of life (late August 2007, about ten days before Michael died). Sandra was quite lost as to what she should be doing to help Michael with his dying and prepare herself and her daughter, Diana, for this anticipatory loss. A half-hour phone conversation started my journey with Sandra on her anticipatory grief and bereavement over the past two-and-a-half years. I have learnt so much from Sandra, who is so willing to share her deep thoughts and reflections throughout the process. She also granted permission for us to film her interviews and the memorial on the beach for Michael, as well as interviews with her neighbours and friends throughout the past two years.

The name of this book surrounds a phone enquiry: *"Where would you like your dishwasher?"* Telephones are becoming increasingly important in our lives. They can bring people together, but can also alienate the other person on the line. From Sandra's story, I am able to understand what an expatriate wife might go through in cancer diagnosis, treatment, relapse, end-of-life and bereavement in Hong Kong, where the dominant language is Chinese. Fortunately, medical professionals operate in English as well as Chinese in Hong Kong, and its people enjoy a very high standard of medical care in public hospitals.

Trained as an organisational psychologist and psychotherapist, Sandra articulates her thoughts, feelings, ambivalence, conflicts and struggles meticulously and succinctly. She so graciously presents her pains and gains, suffering and inspiration, confusion and reflections throughout the process of being the spouse of a husband with a deadly diagnosis in a strange land. This book is the true story of Michael Keys in his path of cancer, death and dying, as well as that of Sandra and Diana in their bereavement journeys.

COMPASSION

In an e-mail Sandra sent me a year later, after going through the transcript of her first interview, held three days before Michael's death, she wrote:

> You tell Diana and me about how to transform this experience into our future work and career—drawing on our understanding of people's pain and suffering to help in future. I see this as part of the next step that you have already labelled for me/us in the form of how to integrate Michael's legacy into our lives.

By embracing the precious last moments in life and continuing the legacy of love for the patient and family members, individuals may begin to look for spiritual growth and transformation through their own dying process, and that of their loved ones. The Chinese word for 'compassion' is composed of two characters meaning 'loving-kindness' and 'sadness-empathy'. This book is certainly a book of compassion and legacy. Many bereaved persons, such as Sandra, have reported a greater compassion for others in pain because of their spiritual insights and reflections developed through their journey of suffering.

BITTER-SWEETNESS

It is easy for individuals to be totally absorbed into the pain and grief of loss, and lose sight of happy moments and sweet times that were deposited into their emotional bank account. No pain, no gain. There are gains behind the face of loss if we search hard enough. Accept the bitterness and pain in the loss, and actively look for the sweet aftertaste from bitterness. We may even be able to convert the experience of loss into a bitter-sweet journey of unconditional love and forgiveness. In Chinese medicine, bitterness is the best medicine. Experience of loss and pain can lead to life lessons and the transformation of personal goals to become a more loving and compassionate person.

In one of our interviews, Sandra recalls the 'bitter-sweetness' of sharing a bottle of wine—that of their wedding anniversary—with Michael. The wine, which was brought to Hong Kong from the UK years back, had gone sour, and yet:

> [It] was so beautiful, [so] moving. So that moment of the not-tasty wine gave us a sharing of a beautiful memory, which also makes me want to talk about what you've labelled [as] 'bitter-sweet'.
>
> But for me, as I was just trying to say to you, you are describing beautiful, kind of fun things, but where we are at right now, I don't know we can experience those as fun, because actually what we feel is just so—there's not even one word—sad, angry, distressed. For me, when you said 'bitter-sweetness', the 'bitter' fitted, because my feelings could come under the category of bitter, just lost in that bitterness...
>
> And now I'm feeling pure love to be able, after fourteen years of marriage, to be faithful to all wedding vows. To realise that now I am being faithful to the final one—and that's actually as loving as any of the others, but in a very different way. And I didn't expect that. I didn't expect to feel just the depth of love amongst all this other pain.

The first year of bereavement for Sandra was tough. She mobilised her utmost personal, familial, social and communal resources to cope with the legal, financial, emotional, cognitive and physical demands. She organised short trips for herself and Diana during long holidays, as festival seasons can be emotionally devastating. Sandra kept a diary of her experiences and started writing this book after the anniversary of Michael's death. The goal of this book is to share her experiences and path of recovery. The writing and publishing of her story is a way to celebrate the life of Michael and their love for each other. The preparation of the book was a healing process for Sandra as the retelling of her experiences through writing, rewriting and editing helped her realign the facts and put events into sequence to develop a greater sense of coherence in what she had gone through during these very stressful but memorable moments of her life.

I enjoyed reading Sandra's story and would strongly recommend it to you all. As the death of a spouse was found to be the most stressful event in life, all married people should prepare for their bereavement besides preparing for their own death. I have shared video clips of Sandra's interviews in the 2009 ADEC (Association of Death Education and Counselling) Annual Meeting in Dallas from a professional perspective. Sandra's experience was shared in a case story as a chapter in the book *In Celebration of Life: A Self-help Journey of Preparing for Death and Living with Loss and Bereavement* (Chan, C.L.W. et al. Centre on Behavioral Health, University of Hong Kong, 2009). I am sure that her own book will be even more helpful, as it is a first-hand report of actual events, through the process of shock from a deadly diagnosis; uncertainties of surgery; torture from chemotherapies; hopelessness and helplessness in the final stage of despair and death; worries about finances; absorption into pain of loss and self-pity; the long process of recovery through endless and sleepless nights during bereavement. Every family has its own stories; I hope Sandra's book can start us all in writing the narratives of our own lives.

Professor Cecilia Lai Wan Chan
Director, Centre on Behavioral Health
Si Yuan Professor in Health and Social Work
Professor, Department of Social Work and Social Administration
The University of Hong Kong

16th January 2010

Introduction

Learn how to live and you'll know how to die;
learn how to die, and you'll know how to live.

Morrie Schwartz
Tuesdays with Morrie

Storytelling is one of the ancient art forms. It is practised all over the world, and in almost every known language there is a word or phrase for 'storyteller'.

As I now tell you my story, I think of tribal cultures, some of which I have sat with before in my travels. I imagine us sitting around a campfire together as you listen to my tale and as I, in turn, look forward to hearing yours.

My story is one that takes us through my husband's successful fight to become probably the world's longest living survivor of a very rare form of heart cancer, cardiac leiomyosarcoma, through his subsequent dying and then onwards through my grieving.

Through narrating our true family story, I aim to encourage and inspire readers to realise that open communication, sharing, learning about and accepting aspects of death and dying teach us all valuable lessons in living that are simply too important and precious to keep hidden by taboo in frightening corners of our existence. We teach so many subjects in life—why not this one? Ours is a life-affirming story.

In his book *Staring at the Sun: Overcoming the Dread of Death*, the eminent psychotherapist and author Irvin D. Yalom writes of 'the awakening experience'. The period of time that I share with you is certainly an 'awakening experience' for us. Our lives and the path that we thought we were on, indeed had planned to be on, are turned completely upside down overnight and without warning. How often do we hear of this happening to others? We hear it often—and it happened to us.

Words do not easily describe what it takes to become one of the world's longest living survivors of cardiac leiomyosarcoma and it is my personal honour to share Michael's achievements with you. Michael secured the respect of every medical professional whom he ever met, including some of the world's top surgeons, right up until the very end of his life. His story is published in medical journals. His legacy is already informing the treatment of cardiac leiomyosarcoma in years to come.

Yet it is not only Michael's incredible achievements that I want to introduce you to, but also Michael the man, the man whom his family, friends, colleagues and Diana, our daughter, and I have loved in person and will continue to love in memory. It is also my story, our daughter's story and the story of an extraordinary international network of people who are involved in our living and loving. In narrating our story, I write openly and honestly as a woman, as a wife, as a mother, as a widow, as someone with ten years' professional training in psychotherapy underpinned by ongoing personal work, and as someone with twenty years' experience of working in corporations in management and human resources development. I do not aim to provide any 'right' answers; my goal is to tell a story and, in so doing, I invite you to walk by my side in reflecting on, creating and sharing your own life story. The process of writing this book is an inherently creative and therapeutic one for me, and indeed the use of narrative writing in this way is also intended to be a tool for practitioners to use in teaching case studies.

In his book *Lessons of Loss: A Guide to Coping*, Dr. Robert A. Neimeyer writes:

> If life is viewed as a story—albeit one we write with our actions and commitments as well as with words—then loss can be viewed as disrupting the continuity of this narrative, posing the threat of radical incoherence in the pre- and post-loss account. Like a novel that loses a central supporting character in a middle chapter, the life disrupted by bereavement forces its 'author' to envision potentially far-reaching changes in plot in order for the story to move forward in an intelligible fashion.

Despite the fact that death is one of the only certainties in life, it remains a taboo topic and one that people do not like to face. I like to think that it is through more sharing, discussion and storytelling that we might bring this topic out into the open, to feel less frightened of it and to support each other with experiences and learning.

You will see that my written words are interspersed with quotations from songs. These songs emerged naturally in my mind as I was writing my book, with the music both deepening and easing my emotional connection with my words, as if like the flow of an ever-changing mountain stream: at times with fast rapids crashing forcefully against the rocks and, at others, calm and gentle like a mill pond. The writing is an inherently therapeutic process for me and I have downloaded all the songs onto my iPod to listen to whilst reading the story.

So imagine now, if you will, that we are resting by the campfire together as friends as the evening sun is setting, and as my story begins...

In the Beginning
1992

Who can say where the road goes,
Where the day flows?
Only time...

Enya
'A Day Without Rain'

This is a true story of ordinary people, of an ordinary family. We are neither rich nor famous. We are ordinary people who find ourselves suddenly, and without warning, facing extraordinary circumstances. If we can move in such an unexpected direction in our lives, then, if you have not done so already, so too can you.

* * *

Michael and I first meet around March 1992. I have recently started a job as a Training Manager working with the National Health Service in London. My colleague Fiona, a lovely Scottish woman, tells me that she would like to introduce me to a close friend, Michael, whom she thinks I will like. We all meet in a Central London pub. There is an instant attraction between us. Michael is six feet tall, with dark, wavy hair and a strong Glaswegian accent that I find really attractive. My own roots are Northern English. I am 28 and he is 30 years old. Michael was born on 22nd March 1961; my birthday is on 21st January 1964. It's a traditional tale of boy meets girl—a love story.

I recall the scene of our meeting vividly: the smells and sounds of the London pub, the noise and music, the excitement of my feeling of attraction to Michael, watching his eyes and lips, absorbed in the sensation of being close to him.

I am often amazed by how real some distant memories can be, when at other times I can barely remember what I did last week. I still remember our first kiss as if it were yesterday: we are dancing in a London gay club with my flatmates Steve and Martin and it is important to me that Michael feels at ease with them. I can hear the distant strains of ABBA music (yes, even in the 1990s!) as I write.

We are having a lot of fun; I dance and observe Michael, as if in slow motion, across the dance floor. I am lost in his eyes. I watch him attract quite a bit of attention from other men. Yet, as we are leaving the club, he takes the opportunity to pull me down onto his knee to kiss me and I feel delightful sensations of arousal at our first kiss: I feel very happy in that moment, as a straight woman, to learn that he definitely isn't gay!

We start to go out together and develop strong mutual feelings, slowly getting to know each other and learning about the life dreams that we share. We fall in love. Michael asks me to marry him on 20th September 1992. I accept. This date is our friend Fiona's birthday and, unknown to us at this time, will also be the date of Michael's funeral back home in Scotland, fifteen years later in 2007. We marry on 6th February 1993 in the cold, misty air to the sound of a piper in a kilt, organised by my sister Alison outside Christ Church Heaton in Bolton.

* * *

Now, it's August 2007, a very long way indeed from Bolton, and I am camping out in the Intensive Care Unit (ICU) of the Prince of Wales Hospital in Shatin in Hong Kong, where I have been for five or six days.

For those of you who don't know Shatin, it is a large urban sprawl which, back in the not-so-distant living memory of our neighbours Paddy and Barbara, was a small fishing village, although the remnants of any village are now impossible to detect amidst the sea of high-rise concrete buildings. Paddy is a recently retired former military pilot who also trained pilots for many years with a commercial airline here in Hong Kong. Paddy and Barbara are strong, exceptionally kind and well-respected people whom I am very proud and grateful to count as close friends, and with whom I spend many a relaxed evening resolving all of life's problems over a good bottle of wine. They are both British-born.

Barbara first tells me of the history of Shatin when she shows me how to drive to the hospital, knowing the area well as their granddaughter has been going to school there for many years. There is still a wide river running through the centre of Shatin amidst all the modern, concrete shopping malls. The Prince of Wales Hospital is one of the main government teaching hospitals in Hong Kong. It is by no stretch of the imagination a beautiful building, yet we have spent so much time walking the corridors of this hospital over the past eight years that, strange as it might sound, it has become a second home for me.

* * *

How do we come to be here?

I think back to 1997 and 1998. Michael and I are living in a small, two-bedroom house between Luton and Dunstable in the UK in an area called Houghton Regis. Michael buys the house before I meet him and I move in to live with him.

Michael originates from Paisley, a working-class area just outside Glasgow in Scotland. His Scottish dad worked in the shipyards when Michael was growing up. His Irish mum moved across to Scotland when they married. Michael is the elder of two boys, his brother William being adopted a few years after Michael was born. Michael studies hard when growing up in order to make a successful career for himself. He goes to St Mirren's Academy until the age of eight and then starts work in Paisley as a quantity surveyor. By the time that we meet, he is living and working in and around London.

Soon after we marry, I support Michael in his decision to retrain in arbitration and dispute resolution. I am working full-time and his desire to study is very strong and important to him. After working for Kier Southern, a large construction firm, for many years, Michael then joins Harold Crowter Associates, a company specialising in arbitration and dispute resolution. Harold offers him an opportunity to work in Hong Kong. Harold is a very important man and mentor in Michael's life. For Michael, it is an honour and privilege to work with Harold, and this overseas job offer fits his life and career dreams.

Unfortunately, at this time, moving to Hong Kong is definitely not my life dream! I have successfully established my own business in the UK, have my closest friends in London and am actively engaged in psychotherapy practice, training and personal work through an organisation called Spectrum in North London that is very important to me.

I grew up in Bolton in the North of England, having been adopted by my parents as a six-week-old baby. I am the elder of two sisters, my younger sister Alison also being adopted (from different birth parents) two years after my birth. My dad, a lecturer in bookkeeping, was the sole wage earner in our family when we were growing up and, like Michael, studying hard was my way to secure later financial independence. I became the first person in our family to attend university when I moved to study in Edinburgh in September 1982 at the age of 18. Michael and I left our family homes around the same age and were independent from then on. I strongly resist the idea of moving to Hong Kong yet Michael does not give up. As an Aries, he has always had stubbornness as part of his nature, although he expresses it in a gentle way, cleverly proposing and arranging short look-see visits to Hong Kong in a way that gradually accustoms me to the idea of this change, and constantly talking with me about the financial benefits that such a move could bring for us. At the time we are stuck with negative equity on our house, both working very hard for long hours yet still somehow building up credit-card debt. We feel financially trapped. I also don't enjoy living in Houghton Regis and miss being close to my friends in London.

Life also brings about its own changes when I fall pregnant in 1998. I always believed I'd never do so. Looking back, this completely irrational mindset seems founded on my awareness of how I was adopted as a baby and raised by parents who could not have children of their own. Naturally I grew up knowing that not every woman can give birth and expecting that this would be the case for me. I never took into account the fact that my birth mother, Pauline, became pregnant at a young age when she didn't actually want to! I first met Pauline on my 30th birthday; Michael was with me at the time. This story and my experience and learning on adoption are enough to fill another book that I would like to write one day.

Michael and I talked many times about having children yet he never took the initiative to move these conversations forward. One evening in our local Indian restaurant I tell him how very important this is to me. Knowing how much my career also means to me, Michael says, "I've been waiting for the moment when you literally grab me by my shirt collar and tell me that you want children." I do not hesitate in grabbing him immediately and very firmly by his shirt collar!

One month later, I am pregnant with Diana. Neither of us expects me to fall pregnant so quickly. We are both absolutely delighted if completely taken aback. This is a natural time of change and I open more to the idea of closing my business and focusing on my new role as a mum.

And so it is that a combination of Michael's influencing tactics and the intervention of Mother Nature prepares the path of change ahead for us.

Arrival in Hong Kong
November 1999

You may find yourself in another part of the world...
And you may ask yourself, "Well, how did I get here?"

Talking Heads
'Once in a Lifetime'

We move to Hong Kong at the end of November 1999 when Diana is ten months old. We are living in a hotel in Wan Chai, the vibrant, bustling, fast-moving, red-light district of Hong Kong full of bars, clubs and lots of bright, flashing neon signs. It is also an area of town near to which many corporate offices, including Michael's, are located.

During our look-see visits to Hong Kong, we have chosen to rent a flat in a residential area called Discovery Bay but have not yet got the keys to the flat. Our furniture is somewhere in transit between the UK and Hong Kong so we are living out of small suitcases.

It really is very difficult living with a small baby in a hotel and I have also been suffering from pre- and postnatal depression so I am longing for some time for rest and recuperation. Any mother of a young baby will know that this is not so easy to find, never mind taking into account the cross-cultural challenges of moving to the other side of the world!

About a week after we arrive, Michael complains of feeling ill; he can't sleep well and is experiencing some trouble in breathing at night. We walk across to a nearby chemist to find him medicine, convinced that he has a cold with slight asthma. My Northern English upbringing does not always lend me to show immediate empathy in such situations, or at least it doesn't at this time. I tell him: "This is no time for you to be ill! There is too much to do! Let's get you some medicine so that you can get well fast!"

Still, no matter how strong my wish for Michael to get well is, he continues to feel much worse. I search through the piles of papers on the floor of our small hotel room to find the contact details for a doctor who will be covered by Michael's corporate medical scheme. There is a doctor in Discovery Bay near our chosen flat. We look out timetables for the ferries to Discovery Bay, which is on an island, and visit the doctor who checks Michael and sends him back to the hotel, with the proviso that he should come back if his symptoms get worse.

They do. On our second trip to the doctor, Michael can hardly breathe and is walking incredibly slowly. Still we don't think that anything is seriously wrong, or at least I don't, as it turns out that Michael is not telling me just how bad he is feeling.

Michael is admitted into a smart private hospital high up in the mountains in a part of Hong Kong that we don't know—which is not surprising: we don't know anywhere in this city! With my blue and white soft baby bag and the constant hassle of carrying a pushchair on various forms of public transport, Diana and I go with him to the hospital. This is all so new to us.

The doctor in charge at the hospital conducts extremely thorough tests and calls us in to talk. I'm still thinking that Michael has a really bad flu. I could not be more wrong.

"We have found a tumour inside Michael's heart."

What? A what? Diana is hungry. I feed her.

"This is extremely rare. We have never seen a heart tumour here in this hospital before. We have called a top heart surgeon and he will be here to talk with you soon."

Time stands still.

We stare at the doctor in shock and sheer disbelief. It sounds like a cliché, yet it isn't. In this moment, all the plans that we have, the direction that we are following, the structure that we think we have in our lives are, in an instant, swept away from under our feet. I know now that any sense of structure is actually no more or less than a thought, and that a 'here and now' experience can come, go and change, as all we ever have is 'now'. Yet I do not know this then and the sense of loss is incredibly shocking. Our world is crashing down around us.

How did this happen? How did the symptoms that we thought

were related to flu and asthma lead to this? How much did Michael also seek to deny the truth to himself and to me? We learn one of many important lessons on this day.

We learn that both we and the doctors look at presenting symptoms, knowing that these can represent more or less severity of illness, and they make a judgment as to how to intervene.

In our experience, doctors vary in their style and choice of judgment over the level of intervention. In this case, the general practitioner starts with the best-case scenario, believing, as we did, that Michael has a bad cold and asks him to keep a close eye on the symptoms to see if they get worse. Michael's initial common cold symptoms are combined with progressive shortness of breath that we consider at first to be asthmatic, due to the completely different climate in Hong Kong.

By the time he is admitted to hospital, his report indicates that there are further symptoms of 'orthopnea', which *Webster's Dictionary* defines as:

> ...inability to breathe except in an upright position (as in congestive heart failure).

One further symptom described is 'hemoptysis', defined by *Webster's Dictionary* as :

> ...expectoration of blood from some part of the respiratory tract.

Michael had not told me that he was coughing up blood; he only told the GP on the second visit. I know that he did not want to worry me and it is also a naturally British desire to want to play down illness: "I'll be okay. It's nothing serious."

How rapidly those initial cold-like symptoms have escalated into a totally different ballpark.

I see how doctors need to make judgment calls about symptoms with every patient. Each symptom brings with it a best- and worst-case scenario. Doctors know this and must intervene somewhere along this spectrum. Our learning is to empower ourselves as patients to be aware of what judgment is being made: indeed to view it as a judgment call and not as a right answer.

Having now experienced so many medical interventions, my personal preference is to ask the doctor to please tell me the worst-case scenario and to check backwards from there. I now also urge each of us, as patients and as caregivers for our family and friends, to take ownership for looking at symptoms from different angles in partnership with our doctors, and for engaging ourselves fully in judgments and decision-making. I really do think that there are few right and wrong answers; there is instead the best judgment given the available information and the skills and knowledge of the practitioner making it.

We meet with the heart surgeon. This is not the same one who later becomes like a brother to Michael. This is the first heart surgeon we ever meet in our lives.

He speaks. We listen, clinging to his every word with sheer desperation.

"Cardiac tumours are extremely rare. The good news is that out of the few cardiac tumours that are found, 98% are benign. We must operate as soon as possible to remove the tumour."

Our relief is tangible. Thank goodness. Let's get this tumour out of him as quickly as possible and move on with our lives.

Our family and friends are living on the other side of the world in the UK; we have been in Hong Kong less than two weeks. We keep in regular contact with them by telephone, yet we—and especially Michael—are very concerned not to cause his mum any undue worry. His parents, like my own, are elderly.

For my part, it is mostly my good friends and colleagues back in London and my sister Alison (Ali) to whom I turn immediately for support, whilst keeping my dad informed about what is happening. My mother who raised me has been severely ill with Alzheimer's and dementia for many years and my dad struggles to care for her. He has enough to worry about without this.

Moving to Discovery Bay
December 1999

"Where would you like your dishwasher?"

Furniture Removal Company
December 1999

It is Monday 6th December 1999, a day etched in time, captured as if in slow motion, one of those days... a day that, quite simply, I'll never forget.

It's a warm winter day in Hong Kong; I feel a gentle breeze on my cheeks as I look at my mobile phone. It is precisely 9am. I know this for sure as I have been counting down the minutes over the weekend, knowing exactly the office hours for our local medical insurance provider, waiting for the moment that I can finally call to set arrangements in place for Michael's tumour to be removed from his heart.

"Hello, hello, I'm calling because the hospital found a large tumour in my husband's heart over the weekend and he needs immediate surgery.

"Hello... hello... no, I'm sorry, I don't understand... Please can you speak English?

"Hello... no... I'm sorry, I really don't understand.

"Please help me."

My mobile phone starts to crackle as I look out with despair across the wall of the Discovery Bay ferry pier. Diana sits beside me quietly in her pushchair.

In the UK, we had private medical insurance cover with a different company that I never needed to use much. The few times I did use it, the first person to answer the phone was always a trained nurse who offered immediate and kindly support. Where is my nurse now? This is the local insurance arm of a large, well-known global company. How come no one is speaking English? What is happening? Why is there no 24-hour hotline? What on earth do I do?

My thoughts and immediate next steps are guided by the arrival of the property agent whom I have come to meet to collect the keys for the flat we have decided to rent. Stopping to change Diana's nappy, I complete the necessary paperwork, engage in business-like conversation and walk with the agent to our new, small and empty flat up on the 19th floor of Brilliance Court. In the interim, I leave a voice message for the GP we'd seen a few days earlier.

He answers my call just as I am arriving at his practice, uttering garbled words of panic, anxiety and justifiable concern. "I can't get hold of anyone who speaks English in the insurance company. The surgeon is saying that if we don't give confirmation for the surgery today then Michael will have to be sent to another hospital as the need for heart surgery is immediate."

After a lot of discussion and telephone calls, the key advice from our new GP rings out loud and clear in my ears still today: "You were brought out here by your husband's company. You should not be handling this alone. Get angry with them now and get them to talk with your insurance company to get an immediate answer."

So, 'stiffen the sinews, summon up the blood...' I march with brisk vigour back across the plaza towards our flat where one of Michael's colleagues is helping me to unpack furniture from the van that has just arrived.

> You know, it has never ceased to surprise me over recent years how songs, words and phrases come into my mind at moments when I am not consciously searching for them.
>
> It is only when, writing down this quote now, that I check back to find the source. At first, I thought

that it was from a poem about a tiger. I now learn that it is a quote from Shakespeare's *Henry V*. The full quotation is:

In peace there's nothing so becomes a man
As modest stillness and humility:
But when the blast of war blows in our ears,
Then imitate the action of the tiger;
Stiffen the sinews, summon up the blood,
Disguise fair nature with hard-favour'd rage:

William Shakespeare
Henry V, Act III, Scene i

I feel moved. I studied this play as a teenager in school with my friend Karen. Now, over 25 years later—as if out of nowhere—I recall the perfect quote to prepare me for my current 'war'. The words of a man who died in 1616 and lived in a very different world from my own inspire me in my hour of need in 1999. If ever there is a time to believe that our words and actions do count and do inspire, then perhaps this is it.

My role in 'summoning up my blood' is actually made all the easier in this case by a phone call I receive en route informing me that the furniture removal company cannot not fit my dishwasher into the kitchen. They ask, *"Where would you like your dishwasher?"*

What? Who cares where they put my dishwasher! Much stronger words than these actually come into my thoughts! Michael is dying. The insurance company won't pay. What on earth are we talking about? In normal, everyday decision-making this might be important and make sense, but now? The absurdity of this moment will live with me forever, putting life choices and decisions into a realistic perspective. I am totally and utterly speechless. I experience myself as if living in a surreal world.

The next phone calls are from the surgeon and a breathless one from Michael connected up to a lot of tubes and pipes in the hospital.

"Sandra, where are you? What's happening with the insurance? The surgeon has just been in here and told me that if they don't get confirmation of payment then I'll have to leave the hospital and be taken into the government sector."

In that moment, images of paddy fields and government hospitals in tents cross my mind. As it turns out, this image could not have been more ill-informed and if I had known then what I know now, we would have chosen at once to move to a government hospital. Sadly, I am limited by the restrictions of my own learning and experience to date and comforted by the knowledge that my husband is, at least for the moment, safe in a clean and professional medical bed. The last thing that I want right now is any more change.

I move onwards to the encounter with Michael's colleague in our new flat. He is busy supervising the removal company. I tell him what the doctor has just told me. He listens carefully, stops unloading furniture and puts out a call to the Chairman, Harold Crowter, in the UK. Harold makes an immediate decision to front the monies personally and to handle the insurance company later, taking this off my hands. We remain, to this day, indebted to him for the immeasurable support that he so selflessly gave to our family at this time and for a great friendship, which now includes standing beside him through his own battle with cancer and his death within a few months of Michael's.

As an important aside, my husband's company, which specialises in dispute resolution, engaged in negotiations and discussions with our insurance company for many months yet finally still did not recover all of the monies. As I understand it, this was because we had not followed 'the dotted line instructions' of some small print over that weekend, when we were unable to speak with any of their staff due to their policies and procedures! Eventually, the go-ahead for the surgery is given and I make my way back to the hospital with Diana. The day is by no means over, yet a critical lynchpin is now in place. As for my dishwasher, the furniture removers were able to take the lid off it and successfully plumb it out on the small, covered balcony.

In Heart Surgery
December 1999

Sail away with me to another world
And we rely on each other.

Dolly Parton and Kenny Rogers
'Islands in the Stream'

In preparation for Michael's heart surgery, we move our home from the hotel room in Wan Chai to the private hospital. 'Home' as a concrete building is an irrelevancy right now, other than knowing how fortunate we are to have a roof over our heads and that many other people experiencing similar circumstances do not have this same privilege. Thinking of others worse off than we are helps me to keep my feet firmly on the ground.

The children's ward kindly arranges for a cot to be placed in Michael's private room. As a mother and wife, I draw considerable strength in us all being physically close.

Michael's open-heart surgery is, in itself, life-threatening. None of us has faced anything like this before.

Michael's father and mother are in constant contact by telephone. Both are elderly and not fit enough to travel out to Hong Kong at this time. My dad simply cannot leave my mum and, even if he could, he has never flown anywhere in his life due to a problem with his ear that he first suffered from when he was in the Navy in World War II. My sister Ali and my friends back in the UK keep in close contact by telephone.

* * *

Before we moved to Hong Kong, a very close friend and colleague in London, Charles, introduced us to two of his close friends, Debra and

Colin, whom we met on the two look-see trips that we made to Hong Kong. Charles's introduction is an act of kindness that looks simple enough at the time, the type of action caring people take. None of us could fully appreciate at that time just how much this thoughtful act would mean to us. Aside from Michael's work colleagues, Debra and Colin are the only friends Michael and I know in Hong Kong when the doctors find the tumour in Michael's heart and our known world falls apart.

* * *

Debra is an American woman who immediately draws on her strong networks through the American Women's Association in Hong Kong, and they lend me the most incredible, unquestioning, immediate support. Women whom I have never met before, but who are close to Debra, offer to take Diana into their homes to play with their children, to feed her and to care for her.

Michael's work colleague, Bryce, comes regularly to the hotel and hospital to take Diana for walks in her pushchair. The bar staff at the hotel, having learned of what is happening to us, take Diana from me to give me breaks and to play with her in the bar. Okay, so it's an unusual playground yet it works: Diana has lots of company and continues to enjoy the kind of contact that all babies do. Strangers of many different nationalities are our extended family. How can I ever fully express in words what this experience means to us at this time?

As the doctors prepare Michael for surgery, we are introduced to a strange new world of medical language and practice. The doctors tell us all the risks in full detail. We learn to value and appreciate this honesty in time, yet, as a new cultural experience and at this time, these words are difficult to hear.

It is clear that the open-heart surgery is serious and life-threatening. Additional complexities, such as Michael's rare negative blood type and the potential limited availability of blood, put even more pressure on an already unbearably tense situation. Asians, generally, do not have negative blood types. Blood has to be ordered through the Red Cross.

As the surgery is life-threatening, we know that we must say goodbye. Diana, at ten months old, is with friends as I say goodbye to Michael when he is pushed away through the surgery doors with the blue surgical hat on his head. We hold hands. We kiss. "I love you," we both say.

I am alone.

Whilst I do not know it then, this moment is actually the first time that we face the ultimate 'goodbye' together.

My only impulse is to find the chapel in the hospital, where I sit alone in reflection. This quiet, spiritual space is comforting to me and affords me an opportunity to stop and to breathe.

I then call Michael's dad back home in Bridge of Weir, near Glasgow in Scotland. It is moving to remember this now as Michael's dad has since died of lung cancer. Hearing his voice so far away is surreal as I cling to a plastic cup of tasteless coffee and look out over the hillsides of Hong Kong.

* * *

I remember the first time that I ever heard Michael's dad's strong Scottish accent and could not understand a word of it. I am sitting in the back of his car as we are driving around Paisley and Glasgow so that Michael can show me the places where he grew up. His dad is driving and talking. I really can't understand him at all, yet carry on politely nodding and smiling.

Unbeknown to me, he is actually saying to Michael in the front, "She doesn't understand a word, does she?"

I nod and smile, politely.

* * *

Debra joins me to await the surgeon. We are together in a small waiting room as he finally enters. The surgeon emanates pride as he hands us a jar containing Michael's tumour. Debra and I stare at him with totally incredulous looks as we hear his voice telling us how the tumour is different from what he had expected and how complicated the surgery was. We both just stare at this glass jar containing a part of Michael's heart.

Whilst it is a common practice in Hong Kong to show the patient and family the body part that has been removed, this is totally new for both of us; in fact, it is a completely and utterly ludicrous experience that we will never forget. We cannot help but simply look at each other and laugh out loud after the surgeon leaves the room. This moment of absurdity provides welcome relief.

You imagine that when surgery has gone well and the patient comes out, then all is okay. I learn how this is not the case. Actually, there are some incredibly tense hours and days as Michael is admitted into the ICU, when it is still touch and go that he will pull through. In the long story of life, these moments tend to be forgotten, yet when living moment to moment, each bleep of the machines can signify life or death.

To our sheer relief, Michael pulls through and a few days later we await the biopsy results. We are feeling confident and relieved that the tumour is finally gone and that life will be okay again.

Whilst I do not know it then, this is actually the first time that we say hello again together after facing the possibility of ultimate separation. We don't talk about the fact that we are saying hello again. Instead we experience this moment with feelings of sheer relief and a strong desire to get on with life.

Our relief does not last long. We learn that Michael is not part of the 98% of cardiac tumour patients with a benign diagnosis. He is one of 2% of that tiny population with an extremely rare form of cancer—cardiac leiomyosarcoma.

We enter a renewed state of shock.

What have we done? We blindly believed the statistics and allowed ourselves to lean on the sheer premise, amidst our shock, that this tumour would be benign. Now Michael has survived life-threatening heart surgery to no avail, as the roots of the tumour have been left in, and he actually has a fast-growing form of cancer. What limited literature that can be found indicates that Michael now has a maximum of six months to live.

Thus we learn the hard way never, ever again to listen only to one side of the statistics. From now on we ask every single 'what if' contingency question that comes into our minds. If only we had known this earlier!

If only the surgeon had been less focused on telling us 'the answer' based on his judgment call, and had instead talked us through different aspects of the statistical equation. I write this not out of any wish to apportion blame, but rather to emphasise the importance of this learning for patients who expect 'right' answers and for doctors who feel pressure to give them.

We do not know if we would have made a different decision in this case as it would most likely have been necessary to 'de-bulk' the tumour immediately anyway. However, we certainly would have felt better informed and potentially less shocked when the momentary cushion of relief from believing that the tumour would be benign was taken so abruptly away from us.

Eight years later, not long after Michael's death, I host an afternoon of 'Sharing with Friends' in our home in Tong Fuk Village that we film with the University of Hong Kong. Michael and I have been open in sharing our experiences with our community and I see this as an opportunity for our friends to share what it has been like for them to live with us at this time. I want to provide an opportunity for them to share their feelings of us it is a new and unfamiliar experience to talk about terminal illness and dying in this kind of way. Many friends comment on how incredible it was for them to see Michael and me in 'control' of our relationships with the doctors right up until Michael's dying breath. I quote directly our friend Boz:

> ...the way in which Michael and Sandra dealt with the surgeons and the doctors, that really amazed me. You know, just how they controlled [the situation]. You guys controlled what they could do... you were actually telling them or asking them if that [was] the best thing to do, and making sure that when they did the things they did... that [it] was really the best thing to do.

Looking back, I don't feel we were in 'control'—we certainly didn't feel like we were in control of anything at this time! Yet I do see how we took charge, how we took our responsibilities very firmly in the decision-making process, and the moment that we realise that the tumour is malignant is when this started for me. I now also see how inspiring our behaviour becomes to others and yet it simply grew into the norm for us from this point on.

Later on, in supporting those battling with cancer, I recognise how much it takes to act from a position of strength in these instances. In this particular moment, which I am now 'freeze framing'— the moment when we learn that Michael has cancer and has only six months to live—a significant part of our natural human desire is to collapse, to collapse into the arms of people who can support and help us. This is part of the shock and a deeply felt response.

In supporting others, I see and feel their utter desperation at the moment they learn that a loved one has cancer. I see how individuals in this situation immediately turn to doctors to get answers, to find the cure — just as we felt and just as we did.

My own response is now different: it is to challenge, to push, to inspire and encourage the people concerned to acknowledge the urge to collapse, to acknowledge the urge to give up, to acknowledge the feelings of fear and desperation, to get support for these and yet to also take charge, to feel the fear and yet to take action, to tap into the drive and desire to fight for life by getting yourself immediately involved and informed, by conducting your own research, by finding resources, by asking questions... In this moment, this doesn't feel like a choice, yet it is one—and it is the one that Michael and I take.

Standing at the Crossroads
January 2000

Standing at the crossroads, trying to read the signs
To tell me which way I should go to find the answer

Eric Clapton
'Let it Grow'

From the moment we learn that Michael has heart cancer, life as we knew it, or rather, imagined it before is gone forever, swept away from under our feet. We were on what looked like a clear path to emigrate to Hong Kong, to settle into a new home, for Michael to start a new direction in his career. Having initially fought against closing my business and moving to Asia, my own fantasies of being 'an expatriate wife', relaxing over cocktails and taking tennis lessons whilst caring for Diana were becoming secretly appealing to me!

Yet I am also now conscious that after being hit by a bolt out of the blue that stops life as we knew it before, the rhythm of life carries on as normal, as if in a dream. A main difference is that we used to look ahead believing that we knew where we were going, that we knew what our next steps in the plan would be. Of course, we actually didn't know at all and neither did anyone else; it just seemed like we did before and now it absolutely does not. Now when the sun rises, we don't have a plan and we have no idea where our next steps are taking us.

I am particularly aware of my responsibilities for Diana's basic care at this time—regular nappy and clothes changing, feeding, play, cuddles and sleep. In fact, it is this basic focus that keeps me sane. Although the rest of my life appears totally surreal, my responsibility for Diana challenges me to be very firmly grounded in the immediacy of the 'here and now'.

Skills that I have learned from my ten years of professional counselling and psychotherapy training are extremely valuable to me at this time.

When nothing around me makes sense, I focus on the tangible factors of my current reality. Learning from practical group work with Marty Fromm several years earlier in my training, I focus on the senses: what I can see, hear, smell, touch and taste. I know that everything else is comprised of thoughts and fantasies, all of which can change, and indeed have changed in an instant. Our vision of the clear future path was always nothing more than a dream, a goal and a perception. Once that thought has gone away, life continues, although in the pain and shock of facing the sudden and drastic nature of the change, it feels like life will literally stop. Indeed, there is also a deep and strong desire for life to stop, to allow us time to get off, to escape, to run away.

In focusing on the 'here and now', I am empowered. I gain strength. As for the rest of our lives, we face a blank canvas not knowing where each step will take us next. In fact, this is true for all of us every moment of every day; it is just that not everyone is forced to look this fact in the face. What is past is already gone; the future is only ever comprised of thoughts and fantasies. It is only the 'here and now' that actually exists. I see it as a privilege, truly learned the hard way, that I now know, live and experience this simple existential fact for real. This reality is not frightening. It can be tough, for sure, yet it also simply 'is'.

This kind of moment of realisation that man is not in control is one where many people, including Michael, turn to religious faith. Our friend Cheryl later refers to a conversation that she and her husband Ed held with Michael:

> ... what Michael got a sense of very early on is that he's in a situation that is out of his control. He told us very simply, and just once, that "I just realised that this is out of all our control and no one can do anything about it." This was eight years ago when the doctors [had] already said that he was going to die. And he said, "So it's just out of my control. I've given in, you know. God's in control, that's it."

Michael always referred to his faith as that of a 'born-again Christian'. His experience of his faith was in what he referred to as 'his personal relationship with God'. His faith was a private and important matter to him. At this moment of learning that he is going to die, Michael holds his faith and trust in God and never falters from this. Yet he also does something more: he takes immediate responsibility as a man to care about what is in his control or 'in his charge' as a human being. To quote our friend, Philippe:

> It's about how he took care of the little things in a very careful way and takes care of the people in a very careful way—and small things matter. When you say 'thank you' or 'I love you' or smile only, you know, it is very important and I think that Michael really took very good care of all these things that he was able to be in control of and all the rest that was outside of his control, he would just smile about, you know, because anyway it was out of his control.

I also take immediate responsibility at this time as well to care for those things that are in my control or charge in each moment. One main responsibility and priority that I shoulder is caring for Diana. Another is caring for Michael. This is a tough challenge as we both face completely unknown and unfamiliar territory. In a way, I face this like any other challenging project, the main difference being that the 'life-and-death' stakes are much higher than any other challenges that I have ever faced before. Michael and I find invaluable strength in our partnership. We are stronger together on this than we have ever been before. We know what matters and what counts! There is no question.

We move out of the hotel-cum-hospital into our new home, the flat we have rented on the 19th floor of Brilliance Court in Discovery Bay, where finally the lid was taken off our dishwasher that was dismantled, reassembled and plumbed in on our balcony like a metaphor for our lives.

We are deeply grateful that Harold Crowter Associates support Michael wholeheartedly with sick-leave pay so that we have some financial support at this time.

Given the rare nature of cardiac leiomyosarcoma, our strategy for Michael's treatment is to work very hard and to open as many doors as possible, as quickly as possible. Harold phones his daughter, who is a GP in the UK. She explains how this cancer is not even in the standard medical textbooks.

The private hospital where Michael's heart tumour has been removed refers Michael to an oncologist who consults with different colleagues. In the oncologist's report dated 16th December 1999, he describes how he has consulted with a radiation oncologist who 'felt that radiation therapy to the heart together with doxorubicin chemotherapy would be cardiotoxic and may affect the patient's cardiac function'.

He further explains:

> The patient has a high-grade sarcoma that would require further therapy. Chemotherapy regimens that are effective in this setting include doxorubicin (Adriamycin), dacarbazine, and ifosfamide and the MAID regimen with G-CSF support has been used with some success in controlling the tumour. In this year's annual meeting of the American Society of Clinical Oncology, there are two abstracts, one from Germany and one from Chicago USA that use high-dose chemotherapy with stem cell support to aim at improving response and long-term survival and I think that Mr Keys should consider this option too.

In layman's terms, this oncologist—who is a specialist in chemotherapy—refers to the cardiotoxic risks of radiation treatment and recommends follow-on chemotherapy.

Alongside this research by the private oncologist, we have been continuing our own networking. One of the founding directors of Spectrum, where I trained and worked in psychotherapy training and practice in London, puts me in contact with a doctor who works as an oncologist in the UK, and she refers us to a top London teaching hospital. I know her already and feel supported to be reconnected with her in this way.

I coordinate the information flow and the consultation process whilst supporting Michael through his recuperation from the heart surgery and subsequent pneumonia—not a minor consideration! We constantly and openly discuss all the issues and he focuses his energies on recovery.

Time is not our friend. We are battling against the clock; the countdown has begun and is ticking loudly in our ears, ringing constant alarm bells!

One of the many challenges we face is the fact that we are suddenly confronted with incredibly complex medical research and jargon, even more so given the rare nature of cardiac leiomyosarcoma, which is at the cutting edge even for the doctors managing Michael's care. Although in one of those strange ways, this works in our favour, in so much as the doctors definitely have a professional interest in Michael's case even though the ultimate prognosis is dismal.

One of the ways we support ourselves is by ensuring that we can understand and interpret all the complex medical information in layman's terms. We ask all the 'stupid' questions and we learn that it is often in the simplest of questions that the truth of the situation lies. Right now, we look at the widest range of treatment options available to us, whilst recognising that none of these is proven to be able to save Michael's life. We want to look at chemotherapy, radiation, further heart surgery and even heart transplantation—and to compare the pros and cons of each option. This is our simple vision at this time.

* * *

It is moving for me to look back at my handwritten notes from this time on now-fading yellow-lined paper. They are like the notes of a child trying to grasp how to engage with one of the most complex medical conditions, from the starting point of looking up dictionary definitions of basic terms such as 'oncologist', what his job is, what he does, etc. To say this is a steep learning curve is a serious understatement, and yet I have pages of written notes that show us climbing this new information mountain together, hand-in-hand.

* * *

Immediately after Michael's fever from pneumonia subsides in early January 2000, we decide to travel to the UK to follow up on referrals to one of the top London teaching hospitals. This is no small decision given the critical nature of Michael's condition. We keep all the doctors in Hong Kong informed of our actions and they fully support our wish to obtain second opinions.

Walking in the Shadow of Death
January 2000

> Death is a vast mystery, but there are two things we can say about it: *It is absolutely certain that we will die* and *it is uncertain when or how we will die.* The only surety we have, then, is this uncertainty about the hour of our death, which we seize on as the excuse to postpone facing death directly. We are like children who cover their eyes in a game of hide-and-seek and think no one can see them.
>
> Sogyal Rinpoche
> *The Tibetan Book of Living and Dying*

We pack and arrange flights to London. On our way to the airport, standing together with Diana in her pushchair awaiting the airport bus in Discovery Bay, I feel as if a dark cloud has descended upon us despite the warm day. I look out to sea and see only grey skies, although they are actually fairly blue. I no longer know if we will ever see Hong Kong again or where this path in our lives is now taking us. We know for sure that we have been told that Michael is likely to die very soon; we just don't know when. Perhaps the closest description that I can offer for this moment is that I literally experience myself as if walking in 'the shadow of death'.

Describing my experience in this way reminds me of its biblical origins:

> Even though I walk
> through the valley of the shadow of death,
> I will fear no evil,
> for you are with me;
> your rod and your staff,
> they comfort me.
>
> Psalm 23:4 (New International Version)

And it is here in my story that, with the greatest of delicacy, I seek to open up sharing and discussion about religious and spiritual beliefs. I tread delicately as, in my experience, people tend to hold particularly firm views and have strong emotional reactions about religion. I would like you, my readers, to feel comfortable listening to my story, whatever beliefs you hold, whether these are similar to or very different from those of Michael; we also hold different beliefs from each other. Since our beliefs greatly inform our relationships with living and dying, not to discuss them here would be something of a cop-out on my part, so I've decided not to shy away from doing so.

If we look at the definition of the word 'belief' in the *Collins English Dictionary* we find: '1) a principle, proposition, idea, etc., accepted as true, 2) opinion; conviction, 3) religious faith, 4) trust or confidence as in a person or a person's abilities, probity, etc.'

One of the aspects of belief that I think about is the fact that it is a thought, an opinion, an idea, yet it is one that is more deeply held than other thoughts an opinion, an idea, yet it is one that is more deeply held than other thoughts and opinions, and, therefore, accepted as true. In my experience, beliefs are most strongly held when people hold them to be truths.

In reflecting on beliefs and how these form us, I would like to include consideration not only of religious and spiritual beliefs, but also cultural ones. All of these factors have a deep impact on our personal as well as our societal relationship with death and dying. In Hong Kong, for example, it is common to find hotels with no fourth floor as the number four signifies death. The market value of your home would also fall considerably if someone were to die at home, and thus people avoid this. In contrast, in the UK, Macmillan Cancer Support was established to provide palliative care to individuals dying of cancer, to support them in the comfort of dying in their own homes. This is believed to be a positive, rather than a negative, experience. Hence, beliefs differ considerably and shape and form us, sometimes in ways that are so deeply ingrained that they are initially beyond our conscious knowledge and understanding.

When I hold the 'Sharing with Friends' group that I mentioned earlier it is the first time we engage together in discussion of this kind on this topic and it is wonderful and eye-opening to learn from each other and to look at our different beliefs in the light of day, even if doing so feels strange and uncomfortable at first.

As I share my story, I'll seek to be open in talking about Michael's and my beliefs. Please, however, bear in mind that my beliefs are not fixed: they continue to be shaped and formed even as I write. Michael and I held very different beliefs, whilst at the same time loving and respecting each other very deeply. Neither of us had any desire to convert or change the other; rather we always found common interest in exploring and understanding our differences and in being open to learning from each other, albeit whilst sometimes engaging in heated argument! It is in this same spirit of shared love and respect that I ask for us to move forward together in any discussion that emerges on this topic.

Michael held a strong personal relationship with God that he honoured right up until the end of his life. He considered his religious beliefs to be a private matter.

As for my part, I was raised as a Christian, have studied existential literature and humanistic psychotherapy, and have a passion for learning that I hope to hold until I die. This includes learning from different religions and cultures, and understanding how these shape each of us. Ultimately, I believe that we 'are' and that when we die, we 'are not'.

To quote Irvin D. Yalom, currently in his seventies and facing his own dying:

> God, as formulated transculturally, not only softens the pain of mortality through some vision of everlasting life but also palliates fearful isolation by offering an eternal presence and provides a clear blueprint for living a meaningful life.

Irvin D. Yalom
Staring at the Sun: Overcoming the Dread of Death

Religious beliefs provide a wonderful source of comfort for many people, including Michael. For others, religious beliefs may become shattered when they face traumas in their lives. For my part, at this point of time, whilst open to the concept of spirituality, I don't choose to follow one particular religious blueprint for 'living a meaningful life'.

When I experience myself 'walking in the shadow of death' as we return to London to seek advice from one of the top teaching hospitals, I am deeply in touch with my fearful isolation and I am reminded of two other times in my life when I have felt a similar depth and poignancy of emotion.

One of these times is when I was experiencing the ending of a long-term relationship with a man whom I loved very much. At this time in my life I purchased a small book on Jungian psychotherapy when I was attending a conference in Zurich, and I quote from it now:

> Whenever we find ourselves in a sea of passion or an abyss of suffering, we are prey to powerful unconscious forces. How we may either drown in these energies or harness them is the subject of this book.

Aldo Carotenuto
Eros and Pathos

Finding myself swimming in, at times drowning under, and learning how to harness powerful emotions is also a subject of my life.

Another time that I have a similar experience is in the final approaches to, during, and for some months after my daughter Diana's birth, at which time I feel not only connected to giving birth but also to feelings of dying. I feel concerned by my emotional response at this and keep in close contact with my GP to monitor and treat postnatal depression.

Hence I immediately question now, standing at the Discovery Bay bus stop, whether I am experiencing depression and make a note not only to look after myself with great care but to keep in regular contact with my GP.

Whilst taking pains to treat depression with respect, I also experience deeper, multilayered learning as I walk in 'the shadow of death'. Birth and death are the ultimate beginning and ending. To give birth is the deepest level of transformation for any woman. Any change necessitates a process of renewal: giving up the old (ending) and embracing the new (beginning). The processes of ending a long-term relationship, giving birth to Diana, and now facing Michael's impending death evoke similar emotional responses in me.

* * *

In terms of my personal history, I was handed away for adoption at the age of six weeks old and, as such, my first pre-verbal experience of birth is one of abandonment. When giving birth to a child, there is a depth of connectedness between mother and baby, one beyond words or the conscious mind.

In giving birth to Diana, I am reconnecting emotionally with my own birth. This process involves release of old painful emotions as well as, indeed most often, precedes the integration of new ones such as increased happiness. I experience this as part of a deep therapeutic healing process.Another significant fact is that, whilst totally unknown to us on any conscious level at this time, Michael is in fact dying over the same period of time that Diana is being born. Diana is born on 12th January 1999. Nine months later, less than two weeks after we arrive in Hong Kong, the tumour in Michael's heart measures

8.4cm × 3.6cm. Over the period of my pregnancy and Diana's birth, Michael's tumour was growing and he was starting to die. I now believe that I was aware of Michael's dying, on an unconscious level. I just didn't understand this at the time, as the onset of his cancer was neither visible nor part of our conscious understanding.

* * *

I cannot simply describe my experience as we leave Hong Kong to see the specialists in the UK but, for sure, it is a deeply emotional and traumatic time as I shuttle between beginnings and endings, between the ultimate beginning of Diana's birth and the ultimate ending of Michael's pending death.

From the moment Michael is handed a medical 'death sentence', we are both consciously and equally aware of his dying as we are aware of his living. We no longer have the luxury of hiding behind the belief that we will naturally live through to old age. Yet, and this is now a source of considerable interest to me, we focus most of our attention on his living.

Of course, this is natural. Michael doesn't want to die. I don't want Michael to die. Diana is only nine months old; I don't want her to lose her dad. No one we know and love wants Michael to die. And so it is that we start the ongoing fight for his life. Yet, the simple truth for all of us, not only for Michael, is that he is—that we are also—dying; it's just that we don't want to think or talk about this.

> I recently had the honour of meeting a very lovely woman, Jodi-Ann, who has been diagnosed with cancer. I tell her our family story and offer her my assistance. A main source of support that she asks from me is to talk with her about her fears of dying. She says, "Everyone wants me to feel positive, yet I don't feel positive. I don't know whether this treatment will work or not. Yet, I don't dare say this, as it might jinx the outcome."

Her words resonate so deeply with me, as I know this same experience was true for Michael and me. From the moment we learn that he has cancer, we both have thoughts in our mind about him dying, yet we don't want to talk about them. We share a similar fear to my new friend: if we talk about this, it might come true. I see now how this is somehow inherent in our cultures and belief systems, even though this woman and I are of different nationalities. This thought, which we have shared, is actually nonsense, as death will come true; it will happen, whether or not we talk about it.

There are some wonderful, indeed world famous, books about the stories of inspirational survivors of cancer, such as Lance Armstrong's incredible *It's Not About the Bike: My Journey Back to Life*. I read this sometime after Michael's death. I adore it. I read it from cover to cover and could not put it down.

I am so conscious now of how keeping these truths hidden places so much stress on us all. For the cancer sufferers forced into sudden conscious awareness of their dying, they are also under some pressure to be positive, to fight to ensure their best chance of survival, as this is what people who survive do. The truth is, there are also millions of people, including my husband, who do their absolute best to be positive and to fight (and who in Michael's case becomes one of the world's longest living survivors), yet still die — just as we all do.

Being positive is not a panacea for cancer survival— if it were, then we would have a cure for these diseases. And, if not handled with delicacy and care, 'being positive' can actually be a message that becomes a rod for people to hit themselves with. I now feel so strongly about this that I question whether it is not actually one of man's basic human rights to feel, and to have scope to express, the full range of our emotions in the face of our imminent dying. The more we keep these truths, these facts of life, hidden, the more we are each condemned to carry our own private fears alone.

And so it is, with the topic of 'living our dying' in our faces, undeniable, ever-present, that we walk through Michael's battle with cancer as a family.

Arriving in London
January 2000

Nobody's helpless, although
I've never felt this helpless before

Del Amitri
'This Side of the Morning'

I remember back to the summer of 1992 when Michael and I are falling in love. I am 28 and Michael is 31 years old. I picture summer days spent with Michael driving me around the Bedfordshire countryside and up to the Dunstable Downs to fly kites. I hear his music playing loudly with the windows down. One of the bands that Michael loves is Del Amitri. I cannot listen to a Del Amitri song without thinking of Michael and of this time, now with a sense of melancholy, then of carefree happiness. Michael shares stories with me of growing up as a child in Glasgow listening to Gerry Rafferty playing through his bedroom window, of walking his dog up on the Braes, of the Glasgow Barras market, of his family and childhood. I picture the red-brick tenement buildings as I now also see them in the picture frames on the wall in the home of our Scottish neighbour and friend, Ian.

I specifically recall Michael's friend, Deef, sending him a new Del Amitri tape that he really wanted to play to me. There is one track, 'The First Rule of Love', that we play over and over again with a real sense of frustration as the tape ends just before the end of the song and we really want to hear all of the words.

You'll grow comfortable together
You'll start to fit like hand and glove

Del Amitri
'The First Rule of Love'

We fall in love to this song.

* * *

We are not in Dunstable now. Instead, here we are in Fiona and Salomie's home in Wimbledon, in early January 2000, feeling both the winter cold and the ever-present chill of Michael's impending death. In moments such as this one, it does not take much for me to start to be consumed by feelings of helplessness that risk invading every cell of my being. Yet I have learned that at times when I face considerable challenges, there are also other emotions inside of me, one of which is a sheer determination to fight.

At this particular time we risk Diana's first birthday celebrations passing us by amidst the trials and tribulations of Michael's illness. We lit a candle for her in the hospital before we left Hong Kong, yet this seems so little for such an important event that we are really determined to enjoy together. Translating razor-sharp determination into action, we instead celebrate being together at this important moment and plan a dinner with a small group of our closest friends in a local Indian restaurant in Wimbledon, as Michael adores Indian food. Thus, we have a rather different child's party that I will never forget, as we can never re-create it or gather together this same group of friends again.

Diana's first party is also etched forever in her memory as we have talked about it so often in the family. She has grown up with a keen liking for spicy food that is so different from the 'plain meat, boiled potatoes and two veg' cooking her parents were used to in Scotland and the North of England. We always tell her of the important role her daddy played in influencing her future tastes, and she, in turn, shares this story with her friends.

We all love to hear it: after all, our decision to create her in the first place was sealed in an Indian restaurant, too!

* * *

As the years pass by, I continue to invest much energy in planning and organising Christmases and birthdays for Diana and Michael. I do so often in the face of all kinds of trials and tribulations, determined not to allow them to spoil these precious times. I have to push myself to considerable lengths to find the strength for this, as the planning and organisational tasks have mostly fallen on my shoulders.

Recently, Diana, who is now ten, asked me, "Mummy, which do you prefer—Christmas or birthdays?"

I reply, "I don't know. I think Christmas. How about you?"

Diana sighs. "It's so hard to say as they are both so special and exciting."

I feel immense pride well up inside me to know for sure that, despite all the traumas we have faced as a family, our work to protect special occasions for Diana over the years has been successful, her memories infused with the natural excitement, joy and magical wonder of any happy child. I know that this goal has not been achieved lightly and yet it has been achieved, and that is so wonderful.

As Diana grows up we talk with her openly about her dad's illness, always selecting our words and tone of voice cautiously, yet taking great care to ensure that we do not keep secrets from her. We engage and involve her in understanding his illness and in being with him when he is sick and in hospital. We want her to see how this is a normal, although painful, part of life. We believe that facts conveyed in a simple, gentle way to her as a child are less frightening than secrets. She always listens attentively, responding in an open, loving and caring way, sharing her questions, thoughts and feelings with us. In this way, we integrate the knowledge of his illness gently into her life, as part of her life yet not the whole of her life. As such, she is able to also enjoy the freedom of her childhood.

* * *

On the medical side of things, we now have meetings at a top London teaching hospital with two senior oncologists, one specialising in radiation treatment and one in chemotherapy.

Radiation or Chemotherapy?
January 2000

> When someone is suffering and you find yourself at a loss to
> know how to help, put yourself unflinchingly in his or her place.
> Imagine as vividly as possible what *you* would be going through if
> you were suffering the same pain.
>
> Sogyal Rinpoche
> *The Tibetan Book of Days*

Both doctors agree that Michael is at risk both from local recurrence
and distant metastasis (spread). They advise that:

> It would be prudent to administer radiotherapy, applying some
> caution to the total dose in view of the possibility of long-
> term morbidity... He would tolerate radiotherapy easily but the
> concern surrounds late cardiac morbidity.

In layman's terms, this translates as: we recommend radiation
treatment as a prudent follow-up to the surgery, yet there is a risk
that Michael might die from the treatment, as it is toxic to the heart.

With regard to chemotherapy, the considerations are more complex.
Leiomyosarcoma is not always chemo-sensitive and what evidence
is available regarding adjuvant chemotherapy suggests that it may
improve the disease-free interval, but not necessarily improve survival.

This means the doctor recommends follow-up chemotherapy,
which might prolong the time Michael is free from cancer, yet with no
proven evidence that it will help his ultimate survival.

After absorbing the medical data, we are both of the clear opinion
that we would like Michael to have follow-up radiation treatment
after this heart surgery. We are also clear that, whilst it is necessary

to get the strongest doses of radiation possible in order to kill the cancer, it is also important to carefully balance the fact that he might be at as much risk of dying from radiation damage to his heart as he is of dying from the cancer itself.

Later, Michael's oncologist sums up part of the rationale for the decision to opt for radiation treatment rather than chemotherapy:

> Adjuvant chemotherapy was not offered because of a lack of evidence on its use and the cardiotoxicity of Adriamycin, the most active agent for sarcoma.

The major question now remaining is where he will have this radiation treatment.

From family and friends in the UK, there has been a constant plea for us to 'just come home'. This seems to be the immediate, genuine emotional instinct of all concerned. This plea fits hand in glove with our desperate desire to collapse, to be looked after, to be cared for, for all of this to go away. Our family, friends and colleagues feel similar shock, desperation and helplessness to us, combined with real love, care, concern and a genuine desire to help. Together, this is a wild mix of emotions.

On the other hand, Michael and I also know that we don't actually have a home in the UK anymore. We have a house that is rented out. Both our parents are aging and battling with their own problems and illness. My sister Ali is fully absorbed in raising her two young boys and without the kind of available childcare help that we have access to in Hong Kong. My birth mother, Pauline, has a full-time caregiver role looking after her sick husband John.

We know that friends and family love us and will do everything possible to help us out, yet we also know that such solutions can only be temporary.

We also have no work in the UK. Michael's job is now in Hong Kong. After working full-time since my graduation in 1986, I closed down my business before Diana was born to support Michael in his career choice to move here. Although we were both working full-time in the UK, we also had negative equity on our house and an ever-increasing burden of credit-card debt. A key part of our decision to move to Hong Kong had been to turn our financial position around!

Interestingly, our GP in Hong Kong, a British man, also encourages us to go home. Michael and I, however, both hold our ground at this time, wanting to keep our options open both in the UK and Hong Kong until we really know which decision is going to be the best. We know how rare his condition is and, this time, we want to ensure that all angles are covered as well as possible.

'Home' for us has become more of a nebulous concept than a physical reality. Our physical home in the UK is now too small for us and is rented out. We don't want to live there anymore. We long ago left our parents' homes. Home here in Hong Kong has so far comprised a hotel room, a hospital ward, and now our newly rented flat. Also, given the rare nature of Michael's condition we really want our decision to be informed by the best possible medical research.

I send our GP in Hong Kong a six-page fax from the UK to keep up the momentum in facilitating communication and the sharing of information. In this fax, I specifically request his help in setting up a referral for us to the Prince of Wales Hospital in Shatin, where he had previously recommended a particular specialist who heads up the oncology team. At this stage I still don't know much about the government healthcare system in Hong Kong, yet we want to find out. I forward copies of all the medical reports from the UK. In taking this action, I feel myself swimming hard against the emotional tide of others recommending us to go home to the UK and yet it feels really, deeply important to both of us that I do so and that we keep all doors open.

With the support of our GP, we are successful in gaining a referral to the Prince of Wales Hospital. We seek advice whilst still in the UK so that we can compare like with like, and make our final decision without Michael having to put his health at more risk by flying again unnecessarily.

Cutting a long story short, the Prince of Wales Hospital also supports the option of immediate follow-up radiation treatment, but with a slightly higher dose of radiation (twice a day) compared to the London teaching hospital (once a day), through a 'hyperfractionated' process. The fact that he can get a higher dose without it coming in one hit is a potential advantage.

Michael and I are sitting on the steps by the telephone in Fiona and

Salomie's home. The central heating is on. The weather is cold outside. We have all the faxes, medical reports and paperwork in front of us.

I say, "Michael, I think that the time has now come to make a decision. I think that we now have enough information. Ultimately, I am aware that this is your life and, as your wife, I want you to know that I'll be by your side and that I'll support you and Diana in any way that you want me to. We can take either step at this stage and we will tackle together whatever challenges face us. I promise you that."

Michael replies, "I know. I have weighed all of this information up again and again in my head. Ultimately, I see six of one and half a dozen of the other and we are not medical experts so we are never going to know. I see how a lower dose of radiation might be more protective to my heart so that I don't die from the damage. Yet I also see how the hyperfractionated approach will enable me to receive a higher dose of radiation treatment, whilst also helping to minimise the risks to my heart. *Having thought about all of this so much, I'd rather die living my life's dream than return home to die.*"

Tears immediately well up in my eyes and I hug him so hard as if to never let him go ever again, and as if to single-handedly will him to live. Our shared decision is made.

The significance of this moment should not be underestimated. In a wonderful book called *Man's Search for Meaning*, the author Viktor E. Frankl describes his struggle for survival in Auschwitz and other Nazi concentration camps. In so doing, he approvingly quotes the words of Nietzsche: 'He who has a Why to live for can bear almost any How.'

Frankl argues that 'striving to find a meaning in one's life is the primary motivational force in man'. In his personal suffering in Auschwitz, his deep desire to write the manuscript for his book was one of the factors that helped him survive the rigours of the camp. He points out how '[t]he meaning for life differs from man to man, from day to day and from hour to hour. What matters, therefore, is not the meaning of life in general, but rather the specific meaning of a person's life at a given moment.'

In this moment, we both find our 'Why to live for'. Michael is determined to get well, to get back to work in Hong Kong and to live the life that he wants to. I am determined to do whatever it takes to support my husband and daughter. We both find meaning in our suffering and through this we gain strength and focus in our living.

We book our flights and return to Hong Kong. Our friends and family understand and support our decision although it is very difficult for them to know that we will be apart. We have both found our 'why' for living yet also know that Michael is dying. We talk less about this, other than when it comes to handling practical matters such as writing our wills, which we do quickly after our return to Hong Kong.

Returning to Hong Kong
January 2000

Take the first step in faith. You don't have to see the whole staircase, just take the first step.

Dr. Martin Luther King Jr

One primary concern on our agenda as we return to Hong Kong is to ensure that Michael is admitted into the Prince of Wales Hospital as quickly as possible for his radiation treatment. We have spent a lot of time travelling for second opinions and time is not on our side. We feel the pressure of this knowledge.

It is now that we also first experience the full weight of the team support in this government hospital in a way that is different from what we have seen of private hospitals. One of the important doctors we meet with is the oncologist, who is managing Michael's radiation treatment and who becomes one of our key supporters. We lean on this doctor for several years until he leaves the hospital and subsequently retires. We are deeply grateful to him for his support.

As the oncologist is setting up the radiation treatment, he shares with us an article published in *CHEST—The Cardiopulmonary and Critical Care Journal*. Harold's daughter who is a GP in the UK had been unable to find any articles on cardiac leiomyosarcoma, illustrating how generally unavailable these are. The doctors at the Prince of Wales Hospital had undertaken literature searches through their medical networks and had drawn out this article for us to read. It is entitled 'Primary Cardiac Sarcoma: A Novel Treatment Approach' (selected reports), published in August 1998 by Movsas, Benjamin MD; Teruya-Feldstein, Julie MD; Smith, Judy RN; Glatstein, Eli MD;

Epstein, Alan H. MD. To quote from the report:

> This report describes the management of a case in a 51-year-old
> white man with a high-grade unrespectable cardiac sarcoma who
> was treated with hyperfractionated (twice daily) radiotherapy....
> The patient is disease-free and functioning well more than 5
> years following this novel treatment approach.

We do not understand all the technical terms but the final
sentence means a great deal to us. All the statistics we have heard
to date indicate that Michael has less than six months to live, and
here we have a man who is still alive and well after five years. We
feel renewed hope as we are reading this. Michael asks if there is any
possibility that we might speak with this patient.

We don't have the report with us at the hospital and Michael wants
to check something as he is undergoing the final medical preparations
for this radiation treatment, so he asks the oncologist to print us
a second copy of it. In this latest, updated version, Michael reads a
note saying that there is an addendum that has been published to
the original report. This is new. In Michael's usual methodical and
meticulous way, he asks the doctors to please get him a copy of the
addendum to the report.

The addendum opens like this:

> Following submission of this report, the patient entered a period
> of accelerated clinical decline due to the chronic cardiopulmonary
> toxicity resulting from his intensive therapy. In March 1998, he
> was admitted to the hospital for a syncopal episode, while in
> the process of being evaluated for heart/lung transplant as an
> attempt to prolong his life in the face of end stage pulmonary
> hypertension. Although he was able to leave the hospital, his
> condition never became stable enough to allow the transplant,
> and one month later he was readmitted for respiratory failure
> with an admission chest radiograph most consistent with
> pulmonary oedema superimposed on severe pulmonary fibrosis.
> He then developed most likely an aspiration pneumonia and
> died shortly thereafter.

We hardly need to understand technical terms: the last three
words say enough! Immediate consultations take place to ensure
agreement on the radiation doses before going ahead. We remain

deeply grateful to this patient, even though we do not know his name; to his doctors for publishing their work; and to our doctors for their constant commitment to research, questioning and working in close partnership with us.

In spite of this sad, shocking information, five years is a much more hopeful goal than the few months which most statistical data indicate remain to Michael.

Our oncologist friend from London visits Hong Kong, meets the doctors at the Prince of Wales, is very impressed with the technology there and considers us to be in very good hands. We deeply appreciate her support. Through her professional eyes we also start to learn more about the high quality of government health care in Hong Kong, where the government has also invested in state-of-the-art technology for cancer care.

Setting Up Home in Hong Kong
February 2000

> Home is where one starts from. As we grow older
> The world becomes stranger, the pattern more complicated
> Of dead and living.
>
> T.S. Eliot
> 'Four Quartets'

Alongside setting up Michael's medical care, I face the challenge of settling into a new country and building a home for my family. Ever caring and supportive, Debra advise me to turn to meet new people at the American Women's Association (AWA), which holds a monthly coffee morning in Discovery Bay for newcomers to Hong Kong. I decide to go, as this coffee morning offers a way to meet new friends and is the first social event that I would have attended. It is held in someone's beautiful home where I meet about twenty or so women.

So there I am sipping my coffee, listening as people start to introduce themselves. I feel comfortable listening to the problems of integrating into a different community, adapting to different food, finding domestic help, etc.

When it is my turn to speak, I feel quite relaxed when I open my mouth: "Less than two weeks after we arrived in Hong Kong, my husband was diagnosed with a rare form of cancer and has been told that he has less than six months to live. He is now in hospital undergoing radiation treatment. We have one daughter, Diana, who is now one year old..."

My words start to falter as tears well up and I start to gulp back the flood, trying without success to regain some semblance of control. This coffee morning is the first time that I speak openly of our experiences thus far in Hong Kong—and I'm not as prepared as I thought I was!

I am living so completely from moment to moment that, until this one, I honestly (I know this sounds unbelievable and yet it's true) have not fully appreciated how totally different my own reality is from that of the other women. In this moment, however, the difference is so evident to all. The whole room falls silent. Everyone looks at me without having any clue what to say or do. No one wants to continue to talk as they find their own problems and concerns suddenly trivial. For my part, I immediately feel shy and embarrassed; I wish that I could take my words back. I don't want to be the centre of attention. I want to find a way to fit into this community and to make friends, not to alienate myself—this might be much more of a challenge than I had anticipated! I ask people to please continue talking whilst I accept hugs, more cups of coffee and mountains of biscuits, valuing the warmth of company.

I know that some other women present that day remember this meeting as vividly as I do. I never set out to create an impact; I simply wanted to make friends like everyone else. The truth, however, does have impact and this matters even if, at the time, it is shocking and no one knows how best to respond or behave. I have learned that this is not a 'bad' thing. I have learned how I touched the lives of others in that moment and how problems that consumed them melted away. Every action has a reaction.

In this case, one of the many incredible reactions is that a group of women from the AWA, who to this day remain nameless, cook additional food when they prepare meals for their own family each evening. I only know the name of one of the women, Annie, as she brings this food to my home every day and becomes a good friend. It is really difficult to express how deeply supportive these selfless acts of kindness are to me. I am a proud, independent and determined woman, for whom it is not easy to lean on others. Yet when I do lean, I feel the strength and love of a community beneath me. This is an incredibly powerful and life-affirming experience, which provides my first step in embracing support and learning to accept it with deep gratitude.

Annie and her husband Steve kindly invite our oncologist friend from London to stay in their home. They and I notice that she does not seem well. I know that she has suffered with bipolar disorder for many years. To my deep dismay, she commits suicide less than a year after her trip to see us. The shock of her death merges into the day-to-day experience of living with dying that we face over these years. Despite whatever traumas face us daily, the process of making friends and settling into the community continues. One of my goals is to meet other mums and to introduce Diana to other children. I start this process by making time to accompany her in the play areas and in the central plaza. I can't say that I am always relaxed when doing so, as I have a lot of things on my mind, yet I hang out anyway.

It is one afternoon while pushing Diana on the swings in the playground at the far end of Discovery Bay beach that I start to talk with Caroline as she in turn pushes her daughter in the heat and humidity. Caroline, as it turns out, has been in Hong Kong for many years and she is open in talking with me. I warm immediately to her. She, of course, has friends in this community and doesn't necessarily need another one, but she is gentle and kind. We bump into each other a few times and gradually she talks with me about a Mother and Baby Group, which meets on Mondays in different people's homes. She kindly invites me to join.

At first, I find it quite difficult to integrate into the Monday Baby Group. I have not needed to make new friends in quite some time and doing so is a process that does not come naturally to me as I tend to have small groups of really good friends to whom I remain fiercely loyal.

The Baby Group brings additional challenges: many of the topics of conversation—buying furniture, making curtains, painting homes, finding baby clothes, even what each of the babies are doing—are not ones I have had much time to attend to over recent months. I move, sometimes in dramatic emotional swings, between feeling so out of place and, at times, frankly jealous of the comparatively 'easy' lives I see other people enjoying. I notice these feelings ebb and flow, allow them to pass, and continue to attend the group.

Gradually, my attitude changes: I feel pleased to learn where to buy furniture and find time to buy some new pieces of our own. When the removal company unloaded our furniture into Brilliance Court on that fateful day when we discovered that Michael had a heart tumour, the removal man took one look at our old dining table and said, "You do know that you can buy real wood furniture here in Hong Kong." He looked genuinely confused as I was signing the invoice and staring at him with complete incredulity, with absolutely no idea just how very close he was to getting thumped! I also gradually relax and value the company of my new friends, who become bedrocks of support. I see all the things that we share and begin to learn more about our cross-cultural differences. With my friend Tracey from this group and her husband Wayne, Michael, Diana and I experience our first South African barbecue Christmas turkey, which is a wonderful world away from Scotland and the North of England! With my friend Annie and her husband Steve, both Australian, we learn to savour the joy of sitting outside on warm evenings drinking wine and listening to Steve play the guitar.

As the years pass, the time spent relaxing with my friends becomes more and more precious to me. Looking back, it is snatched moments with friends, mulling over cups of coffee or handling the chaos of our children's birthday parties that I remember as incredibly valuable and incredibly fleeting. Looking out over the long body of time I see how we have each shared our different perspectives at different times in our lives. Such is the value of true friendship; such is the importance of connectedness and intimacy. Sometimes it is our turn to give and at others to receive, and thus evolves the cycle of living, loving and caring for each other. What is also wonderful is that these cross-cultural friendships grow and spread across the world.

In time, I meet other friends through a Friday Baby Group, especially Lauren and her husband, Julian—who remain close by my side today in Hong Kong—and Gill, who now lives in the UK, and who was able to join me for Michael's funeral there. So, from the basis of true friendship, global community opens up.

As for Diana, she doesn't now recall the names of all the children whom I mention from the Baby Groups, yet she thrived on all the company, fun, playgrounds, swimming and parties when she was young and always remembers closest friends such as Paige. Whatever else is going on in our lives, Diana and I develop a social scene that nourishes us both and that I believe gives us our secure foundation for the future. Baby Groups are replaced by kindergarten, art and ballet classes, and school camps—always, she remains connected with children who become friends. Ensuring Diana's active involvement in all these activities is another key way we keep a sense of normality in her life in spite of the terminal illness that her dad is suffering from. Knowledge of this is one part of her life and it does not stop her from enjoying the rest.

In his book, *Staring at the Sun: Overcoming the Dread of Death*, Irvin D. Yalom talks about the importance of 'connections'. He asks, "If we are born alone and must die alone, then what lasting fundamental value can connection have?" and answers his own question, "Rich connections temper the pain of transiency."

A friend recently sent me a lovely quotation:

A good friend is a connection to life—a tie to the past, a road to the future, the key to sanity in a totally insane world.

Lois Wyse

Amidst setting up home, there is one thing that happens that I seek to forget. Even now I notice myself fitting it into the end of a chapter. Somewhere in the early part of 2000, I become aware of a lump in my breast. I seek to deny its presence to myself, let alone to others. I feel terrified. In caring for Michael and Diana, my own health is way down the agenda. I simply cannot afford to be ill.

Terrified at even the thought that I might have cancer too, I decide to get my breast lump checked out. I don't talk with many people other than Michael and some close friends about this. I quite simply feel overwhelmed and want this problem to go away. The doctors perform a needle biopsy and the findings are clear: 'Left breast lesion—needle aspiration cytology—negative for malignant cells; suggestive of ductal epithelial hyperplasia.'

It is not usual for me to read medical reports that show findings to be clear of cancer. Absurdly, perhaps also naturally, I even feel some momentary guilt about this—why should my report be clear when Michael's is not?

Practically, however, I know that the findings of needle biopsies are not necessarily accurate as they depend on where the needle enters the breast and, even with guidance by ultrasound, there might be malignant cells that are not extracted. Although my mind is not at ease about this, for now I accept the relief of the negative findings from the needle biopsy.

In addition to preparing Michael for his radiation treatment, worrying about my breast lump, seeking to make friends for Diana and me, and settling into our new community, there is another challenge looming on my horizon: the need to earn money—and fast!

Financial Pressures
— My First Job in Hong Kong
June 2000

> Whatever you do, don't shut off your pain; accept your pain and
> remain vulnerable. However desperate you become, accept your
> pain as it is, because it is in fact trying to hand you a priceless
> gift: the chance of discovering, through spiritual practice, what
> lies behind sorrow.
>
> Sogyal Rinpoche
> *The Tibetan Book of Days*

The weight of our credit-card debts weighs heavy on my shoulders.
I am very much aware that Michael might die any day and that I
bear these alone. Up until now, we have been in a position to lean on
Michael's sick pay and we simply don't know how long this will last.
Michael is determined to get well and to return to work yet I cannot
rely on this when there is a 'death sentence' hanging over his head.

I set about finding work. At this time, my official visa for Hong
Kong is as a 'dependent spouse' and, as such, the law permits me to
work, so the question is: what work and how do I find it?

I had put up such a fight about stopping work in the UK, but then
the dream of playing tennis and sipping cocktails had started to
appeal to me. How fast it was swept away from under my feet!

I start to work in two main areas. One is in the field of counselling
and psychotherapy, to continue the practice that I was running in
the UK. I prepare and give a talk on 'Dream Work' in the City Hall
that people still mention to me today. I also set about networking and
talking with practising counsellors. In so doing, I learn that I do not
want to do this work at this time. The more research I do, the more

I imagine myself listening to others and saying, "You think you've got problems? Just listen to mine!" This is obviously not the most empathic or professional starting point for therapeutic work!

The other road is that of Management and Human Resources Development in which I had been working since the start of my career in 1986. I approach a psychometric testing company that I trained with in the UK and which has a branch in Hong Kong. I approach their Managing Director, Neil, with my qualifications and CV and ask if he might have any work. After a short time, Neil offers me a three-month part-time contract to support him on a particular project that has arisen with a key client. I have my first work break. This is such fantastic news and such sheer relief. I feel so determined to do my absolute best as this opportunity means so much to me at this time.

The project seems straightforward enough and well within my skills and capabilities. I meet and build rapport with one woman who works for the client and introduces me to the project, and we jointly agree on the goals for my work. However, on the day I start work, another woman whom I have never met replaces her, and the first woman then leaves the company.

I set to work with the new client observing and taking notes. By the end of the day, through some comments she makes, I get the distinct impression that she is not happy with my work. I feel sick. I don't know what to do. With my heart in the pit of my stomach, I decide to call Neil and tell him, on the first day of my new job, that the client is not happy.

Neil and I talk again through the requirements of my work project and he sends me some additional briefing papers. I go back to work the next day; the same woman observes me again. During my breaks, I call Michael who is now in hospital starting his treatment. I also stare out the window at The Peak longing for help.

This time, the woman takes me to one side and is overt in telling me that I am not doing what she would like me to do. I seek to take her feedback on board and to change the way that I do things. Nothing works. I recognise that I face a losing, uphill battle.

In the normal run of events, I might take one project not going so well in my stride, although this is also, thankfully, not a common experience for me. At this time, however, in my first job ever in Hong

Kong, with Michael facing imminent death and needing work so much, I hit rock bottom. I don't remember ever feeling so low, so self-critical, and so physically, mentally and emotionally sick.

That night when I finally crawl into my bed, I close my eyes and pray, "Lord, please help me. I no longer know what to do." I feel complete and utter despair and helplessness. I am working so hard, yet every step that I take is harder and harder. Although I do not follow an external religious blueprint in my life, I still at times find solace in prayer. I see this as partly due to the comforting familiarity of a ritual learned in childhood. I also find prayer a kind of meditative, energetic state, in which I emotionally 'let go' in order to find new direction.

When I awake, my mind is completely clear save for the faint words of a song that come back to me again and again. I cannot get them out of my mind and there are no other thoughts in there. The words are: 'Mother Mary comes to me, speaking words of wisdom'. I grasp to find the rest of the words without success. What is this song? It is familiar to me, I know. Why these words? Why now? What are the missing words?

I call Annie from the ferry to work and talk with her about the words of the song. Looking through the windows of the client's offices, working my hardest to deliver the project and calling Michael regularly in-between, I remember the name of the song later in the day: 'Let it Be' by The Beatles. The completion of the sentence in my thoughts is: 'When I find myself in times of trouble, Mother Mary comes to me, speaking words of wisdom, let it be.'

I have the answer to my question totally crisp and totally clear. There is no doubt: This isn't about '*doing*'; it is about '*being*'!

How wonderfully and powerfully obvious this message is.

This powerful response to my prayer evokes my curiosity about the mysteries of the human brain.

Over our time in Hong Kong, Michael and I have benefited from the opportunity, through the Hong Kong Management Association, to study and work with Tony Buzan, a renowned expert on how the mind works and how best to use it. One of the many things I have learned from Tony Buzan is just how much research into the functioning and full capacity of the brain really is in its infancy. What researchers do understand is that there are some differences between the right and left hemispheres of the brain.

On the days when I am able to work from home, I like to watch Oprah on TV at lunchtime. As I am writing this chapter today, by coincidence, which occurs so very often in my life, Oprah is interviewing Dr. Jill Bolte Taylor, a doctor specialising in the brain, who herself experienced a stroke during which the left hemisphere of her brain was not functioning.

She describes how, in using only the right hemisphere of her brain, she no longer had the use of language or any connection to her history or past (she did not know who her mother was), yet she was acutely aware of the energetic patterns around her. She knew when people were lying, even though she did not understand language. She felt energetically whether people were being kind to her or not. Thus, one of her primary experiences of the world was through energetic connections rather than language. She also describes this experience as a state of 'bliss' so calm and peaceful that she had to force herself to come back to 'reality'.

I am reminded of the time when I was close to giving birth to Diana and how it became more of an effort for me to communicate through language, yet I was acutely aware of people's energies. I knew instinctively which people I did and did not want to be around, though it was very difficult for me to verbalise exactly why this was the case.

I question now if there are times in my life, especially deeply emotional ones, when I—and perhaps all of us—function more from the right hemisphere, although we have mostly been taught to dismiss this experience and pay much more attention to the left hemisphere and its concerns with words, logic, linearity, right and wrong, sequence, analysis and lists. The right hemisphere of the brain is involved with intuition, rhythm, spatial awareness, Gestalt (whole picture), imagination, daydreaming, colour and dimension.

In this particular moment of coping with a new job on top of everything else that is going on in my life, my brain brings me guidance through music, through the words of a song long hidden in my memory that I accessed through the meditative, energetic state of prayer.

I do my best to please my new client to no avail. Having kept in touch regularly with Neil over the telephone, I meet with him face to face. I apologise and then burst into tears. I also tell him in no uncertain terms that I do not expect him to honour the three-month contract that we had agreed on, as this was based on working with the client who no longer wants to work with me.

Neil stands by me. Explaining that I have pertinent and relevant skills and experience that can benefit his clients, he honours his commitment to our contract.

Two years later, I rank as one of the top-earning Senior Consultants in the company, working very hard over long hours, providing high-quality services to diverse clients. Neil's professionalism and commitment pay off and I, in return, dedicate and commit myself fully to my work with him, which I continue to do until this day, as we both now run our own businesses in Hong Kong and are close partners. I also continue to have close relationships with colleagues whom I came to know at this time in my life such as Pennie, Vivian and Wendy, who is now back in the UK.

And so it is that I make this painful and dramatic adjustment to working in Hong Kong, a change that makes my past experience of 'fast-paced' London seem like I had been working in a sleepy backwater. I start to settle us all into our home and community in Discovery Bay and to set up activities for Diana.

Heart Transplant or Not?
June 2000

"Lord you said that once I decided to follow you, you would walk with me all the way; but I have noticed that during the most troubled times of my life there is only one set of footprints. I don't understand why you would leave me during the times when I needed you most."

The Lord replied, "My precious child, I love you and would never leave you. During your times of trial and suffering, when you see only one set of footprints, it was then that I carried you."

Mary Stevenson
'Footprints'

As we are setting up life in Hong Kong, preparations for Michael's radiation treatment begin. Whilst the details are being prepared, determining how the radiation will be targeted at Michael's heart, we continue to have some remaining questions about other treatment options—such as further heart surgery or heart transplantation—that we would like to explore.

Michael's oncologist refers us to a surgical consultant, whom Michael and I meet with.

Let's not forget here that Michael is facing imminent death, recovering from heart surgery and pneumonia and has nonetheless travelled halfway across the world and back to consider the widest possible range of medical interventions, because he and we are now fighting with all the strength that we can muster, fighting to save his life. We are living on a cocktail of shock, adrenaline, physical and mental exhaustion, and sheer determination.

The consultant is distant and clinical in his style. We are learning to ask the doctors to give us the worst-case scenario and we are starting to value this perspective, especially as the very last thing that we now want are attempts to comfort us. In this case, however, the doctor, unlike many others of the same nationality whom we have met, shows us very little empathy and understanding. He reads the files with minimum eye contact and tells us that having a heart transplantation is not an option. We have researched information on the Internet and later read an e-mail sent to us by a doctor in the USA:

> If the tumour mass is not over about 5 cm in maximal diameter it can be controlled with xrt [external radiation therapy] alone in many patients. Beyond that size, it's a poker game. I believe that malignant tumours are a poor indication for an organ transplant because the diseases are too likely to progress to justify the expense and potential waste of the precious organs themselves.

While respecting the doctor's decision, we have also read up on artificial organ transplants and hope to discuss this alternative with him. But the consultant has formed his opinion and he wants to move on to his next appointment. His decision is no. We want to talk more. He does not. We don't feel heard.

We are both so upset after this meeting that we vow never to have any contact with this doctor again. It is not that the doctor is in any way wrong; it is the fact that his lack of interpersonal sensitivity is simply too much for us to take at this time.

Anyone who has ever been handed a medical 'death sentence' knows exactly how Michael was feeling at this time. As for the rest of us, we only have the option of imagining ourselves in his shoes. In caring for him, we can better know how to respond with empathy and understanding if we do, even for a moment in the middle of a very busy day, allow ourselves to feel what it would be like to receive that death sentence in a cold, distancing way.

My point in sharing this experience is not to allocate blame; it is to promote shared understanding. In all conflicts there are at least two sides. It is therefore also important for us to imagine ourselves in the shoes of the surgeon. He, like all doctors, has to make tough decisions all the time and works under high pressure. They face patient after patient with critical illnesses, and a bad day for a doctor can be much more pronounced than a bad day for the rest of us—and we all know the stress of busy, bad days.

The conflict here is not due to the surgeon doing anything wrong or because his professional judgments are not sound and realistic. Rather, it is a conflict created by intercommunication, as well as interpersonal and influencing dynamics that are shown to be all the more ineffectual given the intensity of our feelings in facing Michael's imminent death.

By way of contrast, later on in our journey, we meet another heart surgeon to discuss surgical and heart transplant options. Our experience could not be more different. He explains how he has considered and reviewed all the facts from every possible angle. We already know that he has, from his ongoing correspondence and relationship with Michael via e-mail and telephone.

He gently explains to us how he will carefully weigh up the pros and cons of every case, drawing on his skills, knowledge and experience as a top surgeon to give us his best-informed medical judgment. However, even though he is a good surgeon, the outcome will also be 'in the hands of God'. He tells us, "Sometimes all the evidence indicates that the patient will die yet he lives. At others, we have no expectation of any complications yet the patient dies."

It is not the religious reference that is such a huge support to us in that moment; in fact, all three of us in this meeting hold very different religious views and come from very different cultural backgrounds. Rather, it is this surgeon's sheer, open, honest and humble expression of the humanity we all share that is such a relief to hear. He is open not only about his decision-making process and professional judgment, but also about the fact that these may not save Michael's life. To have a senior surgeon summarise this human truth in such simple words: what an incredible relief to Michael as his patient and to me as Michael's wife!

Here is the opposite of the 'God complex', which TV shows and books often talk about surgeons having. Whether one holds religious beliefs or not, no surgeon ultimately holds the power of life and death in his hands. We learn over the years how much Michael's inner strength and determination play a part in his becoming the world's longest living survivor of cardiac leiomyosarcoma.

Even though Michael doesn't receive further treatment at this time, we are deeply touched by this surgeon's humility and we never forget the impact that he had on our lives at this moment.

Michael goes ahead with the radiation treatment, at the end of which, tests show his heart to be clear of cancer. The treatment is successful.

As part of setting up our life at this time, we employ a full-time helper, a Filipino woman who assists us with housework, cooking and caring for Diana, now one year old. We welcome this additional support.

Post-Radiation Treatment
July 2000–August 2002

The dandelion is like 'death', something that no one wants to find in the garden. However, the dandelion is always there. It is beautiful in itself, and it is resilient. It grows in harsh environments and disrupts the growth of other plants.

Professor Cecilia Chan

Michael undergoes regular medical scans and check-ups with close monitoring and wide consultation regarding the ongoing findings of PET and CT scans. The advent of each scan brings with it renewed anxiety and fear.

He recuperates well from the radiation treatment and makes a gradual return to the work that he enjoys so much and that gives him important meaning in life. He is very committed to his work and also to supporting us, his family.

I establish myself in my human resources consultancy work, gradually lengthening my working hours. In time, I build ongoing relationships with my clients, which, in many cases, turn into long-term ones.

I continue to spend time with Diana and my Baby Groups, settling her and me into daily life in Discovery Bay. I also join another women's group that becomes a valuable source of support. Diana gradually grows from baby into toddler and enjoys her life, with lots of contact with friends and being out in the open air. We both love her very much.

Financial pressures continue to bear on Michael and me, and are at the foreground of our attention. As we work, we steadily, with sheer determination, pay off each of our credit cards month by month until, after a couple of years, all this debt is gone. In recent years, I have been watching Suze Orman, a financial advisor, on *The Oprah Winfrey Show* and have read some of her books. Paying off credit-card debt is one of the key actions that Suze advocates and I like to imagine that she would feel incredibly proud of us.

Life is by no means easy and comfortable, yet we do still carve out precious time to hang out with friends, to swim at the Residents' Club, to enjoy eating out for dinner and having relaxing drinks in the sun. In so doing, we retain a sense of normality, albeit with the typical stresses faced by a working couple with a young child, on top of Michael's ongoing battle with cancer. There is no doubt that we remain under considerable stress, yet we are determined, hardworking and focused—qualities that never leave us.

We travel back to the UK to visit family and friends over these years, and some family and friends in turn also come to visit us. William, Michael's younger brother, helps to bring out Michael's elderly mother who manages the long trip to Hong Kong. My birth mother, Pauline, comes out to visit. Charles, who introduced us to our first Hong Kong friends Debra and Colin, visits us with his partner Jeremy, so for the first time, the six of us are together from different parts of the world in our home and for a really special dinner at The China Club.

In one of our family trips back to the UK for Christmas we have a wonderful time staying in a wooden lodge hotel on the banks of Loch Lomond, the site of many fond memories of the early days when Michael and I were dating.

* * *

We'd originally stayed in a small inn on the edge of the Loch and I always remember looking out of the window at breakfast. The landscape was covered with deep, freshly driven snow and as I watched, a robin redbreast flew up and sat on my window ledge. It was a moment that stood still in time, as if we were living in a Christmas card, as I said to Michael at the time.

* * *

The logo that the University of Hong Kong uses for their ENABLE (Empowerment Network for Adjustment to Bereavement and Loss in End-of-life) project is a dandelion because, they say:

> Our experience of living with cancer is of living with the knowledge that the dandelion is always in the garden—that death is ever-present even when we are working desperately hard to uproot and to destroy it. We might get rid of the dandelion for a while, yet we never know when it will grow again. We live with this knowledge and we fear it.

In the years following Michael's diagnosis, we fight tirelessly for his life and to build our family dream, yet the reality of his dying is also in our face. While this is true for all of us, we don't all have to see it. I think of this as both the value and the curse of cancer.

I know that, for me, I fight for Michael's life while I also think of how I shall cope if or when he dies. I don't want to look at this, yet I do. Whilst this is not something that we talk openly about, I believe wholeheartedly that we both do the same.

In our single-minded working to pay off our credit-card debts, we both prepare to make our lives comfortable and to ease the burden on Diana and me in the event of Michael dying. I hold so much deep respect and gratitude for Michael's unswerving love, care and concern for us, shown not least in his incredible determination to continue working hard and to build success in his career.

Once free of debt, we buy new furniture. We do not know how long we will be in Hong Kong, when or if we will return to the UK. I am determined not to return with our old table of pretend wood! Hong Kong is a wonderful city to buy good-quality wooden furniture.

Cancer Returns in Michael's Stomach
August 2002

And he said, "Someday I hope you get the chance
To live like you were dying."

Tim McGraw
'Live Like You Were Dying'

In his song 'Live Like You Were Dying', Tim McGraw sings of going skydiving, which Michael and I don't do after learning of his cancer diagnosis. We do focus all of our attention on what matters to us the most—our family. We take holidays and we celebrate special occasions: we behave like any normal family, yet with full appreciation of the value and fragility of each day.

> With the benefit of hindsight, I wish that we had taken more time out to go 'skydiving'. At that point of time, however, we think more about all the responsibilities that we hold.

Over these past two years I have been living with my breast lump. Regular mammograms and ultrasound checks every six months show no changes in its size yet I remain acutely conscious of its presence. In January 2002, I decide that enough is enough and that I want this lump removed. Whilst terrified by the thought that I too might have cancer, I also decide to face this fear head-on rather than to live with it any longer. Thankfully the lump is benign. I don't even want to think, even now, about how I might have handled any other news.

> I have a wonderful little book called *Feel the Fear and Do It Anyway: How to Turn Your Fear and Indecision into Confidence and Action* by Susan Jeffers. I have had this little book for years and the words of its title always come to mind at times like this one.

Michael and I already have wills in place and the constant facing of medical issues reminds us of the importance of these. Again, we are not going to mess around with such matters anymore. We know how critical wills are, not least because we are living outside of the UK, our country of origin.

Of course, the regularity of medical checks in my life is absolutely trivial when compared with Michael's and it is in this regard that his life definitely differs from that of the norm. In July 2000, Michael's PET scan findings appear relatively clear taking into account the post-radiation effects:

1. The mass seen behind the right atrium in the CT scan now has no metabolic uptake. The finding is consistent with remission of patient's intra-atrial and retro-atrial recurrent leiomyosarcoma after radiation therapy.

2. A generalised diffuse increase uptake is seen over right ventricle and also a mild increased uptake over the cephalic right ventricular/right atrial junction. These are most likely due to non-specific post-radiation inflammatory change, assuming that the CT scan did not reveal any other tissue mass overlying the right ventricle and the cephalic right atrial wall area.

3. Recommend follow-up PET scan in 3–6 months when the effect of radiation would have subsided.

I describe his PET scan results as 'relatively clear' though when reading the above report, a lot remains open to interpretation so these words do not give us any semblance of peace of mind. Earlier scans have not been so clear due to the post-radiation impact. All scans require careful interpretation by Michael's heart surgeon. By August 2001, findings of a CT scan indicate:

> The soft tissue in the posterior aspect of the left atrium and the lateral aspect of right atrium has remained more or less the same as compared with previous CT scans, with consideration in difference in image technology. However, there is pathology going on in the lower lobe of left lung, which has increased in size as compared with previous CT done in October 2000. Differential include radiation pneumonitis, therefore it is important to correlate with the history of radiation therapy. Infection, particularly TB, has to be ruled out. The radiological features are atypical for lung metastasis. Recurrence of leiomyosarcoma in lung veins is however a possibility to be excluded. Bronchoscopy +/- biopsy for culture and histology will be recommended.

Has the cancer spread to Michael's lungs or are these changes due to the pneumonia that he had? Again, we rely on simple terms to help us sift our way through the emotional impact of reading such reports. And reading reports is, in many ways, the easiest part. For Michael, each check, each test involves lying for long periods in uncomfortable machines, having people stick needles into his veins, push cameras down his throat, and so on.

At this time, Michael is in regular contact with his doctors at the Prince of Wales Hospital as well as with a cardiac and thoracic surgeon at a UK hospital, with whom his surgeon in Hong Kong has put him in touch. Michael regularly e-mails him and visits him when he is working over there. This aspect of his treatment is not as clear in my memory, as I am working hard at my full-time job and looking after Diana so am not with him at this time.

Michael's journey is very clear in his notes, however, and in his e-mail to the UK hospital in April 2002 that gives a clear indication of his strong state of mind:

> Hello Dr....
>
> I hope you are well. I am due to have my follow-up scan soon. So far there is no sign of the MRI on CD-ROM; could you please chase this up for me?
>
> Otherwise I am reasonably fit and well and work has picked up here so the threat of having to return to the UK permanently has

receded in the short term at least. There is a vague possibility of a trip [*sic*] the UK sometime in the next few months, but nothing definite at the moment.

I got a copy of the report a few weeks ago and it identified a condition in the left lung, which helped explain my incessant coughing. My GP has treated me with antibiotics and I am better now than I have been for some time.

Kind regards,
Michael Keys

Over time, with no certainty, it appears that the problems noted in Michael's lungs are due to 'post-radiation pneumonitis in the lower left lobe of his lung'. There is '[n]o MR evidence of recurrent tumour' in Michael's heart. Whilst questions remain in some reports, it is considered most likely that neither the activity in his left lung nor in his heart are related to cancer. This is good news and we start to lean on it.Having faced a prognosis of less than six months to live, Michael is living a normal, working life over two years later in April 2002, balancing medical check-ups and treatments with his career.

Such was our commitment to ensuring financial security that when I look back, I see how we became off balance in terms of how much time we invest in our work . With hindsight, I see the fear that drove us. I felt very frightened that Michael might suddenly die and I would have no job, when financial independence had always been important to me and now I had to consider Diana too.

Michael's work, especially since retraining, had become his passion in life, and in it he found that important source of meaning of which Yalom speaks. His dedication to work was most certainly aimed at supporting Diana and me, yet it was much more. His sense of self and his independence as a healthy man was tied up in his work: there he is neither a sick nor a dying man.

Our worst fears are realised and our relative security is once again shattered when Michael is admitted to a private hospital in August 2002 after starting to pass blood. Findings of an MRI indicate: 'There is an abnormal signal area detected in the pylonic region of the stomach suggesting the gastric tumour.' The MRI shows no sign of lymph node or liver metastasis. Intravenous antibiotics are given for possible chest infections due to Michael's fever and cough.

I am reminded again as I write this how easy it is to regard Michael as a 'cancer patient', yet he is also a man—a man with a persistent cough, with a fever and passing blood, a man who deserves to be loved and cared for. 'Michael the man' must endure the onslaught of words that the rest of us find hard enough to read in the medical reports. Whatever he faces, Michael continuously shows gentle strength and great dignity. As our French friend Philippe later says:

> I'm very impressed by Michael. He was always a very cool guy you know and very calm. I mean sometimes you twist an ankle and then you get cranky and this guy got a return of his cancer and he just, you know, he didn't blink. That's really a new definition of cool for me. And not only that, he was extremely elegant in every aspect of the situation. He never raised his voice; he was very careful. I mean that's tremendous elegance. It's dignity.
>
> And the thing also I think, we always have a choice, but I mean he took the choice very far and up to sharing with us . I think that everybody has a part of this experience thanks to him, because he could have been just, not himself and be depressed. Who would not be depressed? And he was not.

I immediately fax the findings from the private hospital to Michael's oncologist at the Prince of Wales Hospital, who responds immediately by referring him to a gastric surgeon. Further scans confirm that the metastasis of the cancer appears to be localised in the stomach:

> Status treated left atrial leiomyosarcoma. The left lower lobe consolidation and adjacent pleural thickening is most likely from radiation pneumonitis. There is a gastric tumour at the pyloric region extending to the duodenum. It appears to be confined and does not have any sign of dissemination.

After much team discussion, Michael opts to go ahead with stomach surgery. Although Michael is no longer under his heart surgeon's care, I send an e-mail to the surgeon: 'Michael is in Ward 3F with stomach surgery planned for Wednesday. The surgeon is checking his heart and lung functioning just now and we would really appreciate your support.'

He responds without question. He walks over to me at one of the rare moments when I am standing in floods of tears outside the block leading to Michael's ward. I feel so grateful for his continued presence in our lives. Undergoing reconstructive stomach surgery after heart surgery, radiation treatment, pneumonia and radiation damage to Michael's lungs is not a decision that can be taken lightly.

Once again, Michael undergoes life-threatening surgery with his rare blood type provided through the Red Cross. The surgery is too complicated for me to explain well in non-technical terms and involves basically reorganising his internal organs—'a partial gastrectomy with jejunal transposition and an oesophagogastroduodenoscopy.' Biopsy findings indicate: 'A high-grade sarcoma with myoid differentiation. In favour of leiomyosarcoma.'

Michael's pathology report states:

> The cardiac tumour precedes this gastric lesion by three years. The immunohistochemical profile and microscopic morphology of the present gastric tumour and that of the cardiac primary are very similar. Furthermore, the intraluminal polypoid appearance is also very uncommon for gastric leiomyosarcoma. Overall, we favour one tumour rather than double primaries. We also think a cardiac primary is more plausible than a gastric primary. Cardiac leiomyosarcoma is extremely rare. Metastases have been reported in the lung, brain and bone.

In layman's terms, Michael's condition remains very uncommon and there is great uncertainty over his prognosis. Michael's oncologist later concludes: 'No adjuvant chemotherapy was offered because of lack of effective cytotoxic agents and clinical data supporting its use.'

Diana, now three years old, and I say goodbye before Michael goes down for this major operation in his stomach. We are both in the hospital with him: this time Diana is no longer in a cot by her daddy's side; she is old enough to cuddle him amidst all the tubes on his hospital bed. We gently explain to her how very ill her daddy is and that he might not survive surgery. We keep our tone of voice gentle so as not to frighten her but we do not hide the facts of our shared life from her. We take a great deal of care over how we teach and share with Diana but nonetheless do so openly. She deserves an opportunity to say goodbye to her dad as much as I do to my husband.

This is the second time that we say a final goodbye.

Michael recovers fast, steadily and well from the surgery.

This is the second time that we say hello again! Once more, we don't stop to label its significance. Instead we feel the sheer relief and move on, wishing for cancer to be behind us.

We care for Michael first in hospital and then at home. After a period of rest he returns to work. Aside from weight loss, he retains all his inner strength and determination in a truly remarkable way.

Another change happens in September 2002 when Debra and Colin say goodbye and move to live in the UK. Not so long after this, their lives also change significantly when Colin is diagnosed with non-Hodgkin's lymphoma.

Life Moves On and Changes
2003–2006

Once you choose hope, anything's possible.

Christopher Reeve

When Michael's cancer returns in his stomach, my day job involves me running Assessment and Development Centres, which are high-pressure events where we put senior managers through a series of tests and exercises to identify their strengths and development needs. These are typically residential. The company that I work for undergoes many strategic changes and Neil leaves, so I am without the boss who has supported me thus far and whom I respect very much.

Michael is also changing his thinking about work, as he has less personal contact with Harold who is now mostly based in the UK. We talk frequently about setting up our own business as this would, on one hand, bring us new challenges and, on the other, enable us both to exercise more choices over decisions and our time, which is so very precious to us.

I would love to say that our decision-making process at this time is purely logical but it is not; it is also very much an emotional process. We both feel intense pressure and are doing our best to navigate all the challenges that we face. At times, though, we are completely off balance and submerged under the waves even if we do seem to find ways to breathe underwater—we are fighting for survival.

Months later, after running seventeen Development Centres one after another, and when organisational changes occur with which I cannot agree, I quit my job—enough is enough. I am stretched to breaking point and I break. I'd like to say that I managed this ending well but I did not. Michael also decides to leave his full-time job and we commit to setting up our own business together.

This bold decision has significant risks. However, we are as determined in this as we have been in all the other life-and-death decisions. We invest much time in planning and our application to secure a work visa is successful. We strive together for what we want; we choose hope. We launch our business on 26ᵗʰ February 2003. I head up the human resources division and continue to deliver Assessment and Development Centre and Executive Assessment Projects. Michael heads up the construction division and continues to work in the field of dispute resolution. I am incredibly proud to say it continues to grow from strength to strength today.

Over Easter 2003, our good friend Kate offers us an opportunity to stay in her home over the holidays whilst she is away. I am writing psychological reports during this time so it is not fully a rest for me. Nonetheless we accept her offer with sincere gratitude at the thought of taking a break. Kate lives in Tong Fuk Village in South Lantau. We have often visited South Lantau and imagined how we might like to live there. As soon as we experience staying in Kate's home, we know that this is a dream that we want to turn into a reality. The tranquillity of a local village by the beach is something that we both long for, a yearning that reflects our desire for more rest and relaxation in our lives.

Michael immediately notices that the China Bear pub in Mui Wo on Lantau Island has a St Mirren football scarf on the wall. St Mirren is the local Scottish football club that Michael has supported since he was a child. Paul, who runs the pub, frequently visits his family back home in Renfrew, where several years later Michael is to be buried.

In June 2003, the findings of Michael's MRI scan are clear: 'No evidence of recurrence in the surgical bed for partial gastrectomy.' An ultrasound of his whole abdomen is also clear.

Once our decision to move house is made, we quickly take action to realise it and in August, shift into a rented house in Tong Fuk. The move is exhausting in the intense summer heat and humidity, and I wonder many times what on earth we are doing giving ourselves this additional pressure. Yet the move seems right and important for us—not least as it affords us much more space. There is also an international primary school in Tong Fuk—Lantau International School. As coincidence would have it, as we are seeking to make decisions about Diana's schooling, we bump into the teachers holding a planning meeting at lunchtime outside The Gallery, a relaxed local village bar-cum-restaurant. We talk to them and they later offer Diana a place in the school.

The Gallery comes to play an important role in our lives. Dave, who runs it, not only cooks great food but has also established a place where it is difficult not to relax and to let off steam—and, boy, do we need a place to do that! As we settle into Tong Fuk, we chill out at The Gallery at least once a week, usually on a Friday or Sunday evening. This becomes somewhere we both feel able to switch off and escape.

I have spent a lot of time in France, including a year working there as part of my degree, and it's where I developed a love for good food and wine that is still with me today. There are few things that I enjoy more than sharing good food and wine with friends, whilst watching the world goes by (or in Tong Fuk, watching the water buffalo and cows that roam wild along the roads walk by). Time spent with friends in this way is an escape valve, a precious time of light relief. For 95% of my life, I am responsible and professional. The Gallery provides one place where I put all duties down for a while and enjoy the other 5%. We usually sit outside as a couple or with friends. We become especially close to Kate over this time. Michael and Dave also enjoy sharing conspiracy theories about life together. In September 2003, Diana starts primary school with Suzy Lambert as her teacher in Primary 1. I talk with Suzy about Michael's cancer and together we support Diana, with me crying without fail at each parents' and teachers' meeting. I don't know what it is about those sessions! My experience of the support provided to Diana and to our family through the school is deeply important to me and somehow the formality of the meetings brings my feelings to the surface. I am strong, hardworking and care for others, yet these qualities are also taking their toll—I am so absorbed in the demands of life that I don't fully recognise the impact of all these stresses on me.

In December, we learn that my mum, the mother who raised me, is nearing the end of her life. The nurses caring for her advise us that it is time to say goodbye. At short notice, I make the long trip to Bolton in the North of England. Other than perhaps an occasional glimpse in my mum's eye (and I honestly believe that this is actually a fantasy on my part) there is no sense that she knows who we are at all, and there never has been on any of my previous visits. By now her Alzheimer's and dementia are severely advanced. My mum has been angry with violent outbursts for many years and even now she displays momentary outbursts of rage, although for the most part, thankfully, these are now under medical control. I say a final goodbye to my mum who dies on 2nd January 2004.

It is difficult for me to separate my feelings from saying goodbye to my mum from the already too frequent experience of saying goodbye to Michael. I can perhaps best describe myself as living in a state of shell shock. Each time I do start to relax a little, there is a new blow that hits me from around a new corner. After facing a very real abandonment as such a young baby, fear of abandonment is—and I am sure will continue to be, even with all my therapeutic work and training—a lifelong area of vulnerability for me. Each of these goodbyes is challenging.

I return to Bolton alone in January to help my sister and my dad organise Mum's cremation. Our family, especially on my dad's side, only really comes together for 'hatches, matches and dispatches' (births, marriages and deaths) and I find it really comforting to be with my cousins at this time, sharing family stories and hugs over cups of tea and sandwiches. I have always loved my cousins and wish that I could see them more. It helps me to be with them, however briefly.

I see people whom I haven't seen for years and who were very important to me in childhood. It is wonderful to see Aunty Joyce and Aunty Edith. My closest friend Valerie, whom I have known since we were both one year old, growing up together as neighbours in Bolton, flies from her home in Brussels to be with me. I also find comfort in liaising with the vicar of the church that was an important part of my life as a child, where Michael and I married and where my mum's ashes, along with those of her parents, are now held in the Garden of Remembrance.

Having moved house, supported Diana starting primary school, faced the death of my mum, and been in the throes of starting up a new business, all within a year, I return to Hong Kong for Diana's birthday on 12th January and for my own 40th on 21st January.

Valerie now flies from Brussels to Hong Kong to be with me again. We have been in each other's lives for so many years that she is like another sister to me. Our relationship with each other is more like that of family than of friends. I love her very much and am godmother to her son, Joshua. Even at times in our lives such as now when we live far apart, there is nothing that I cannot say to her or that she does not know about me. I am so happy that she is here.

I find myself increasingly longing to receive rather than to give, especially on the one day of the year that is about me: my birthday—and such a significant one. My close girlfriends talk with me in the months leading up to my 40th, asking how I would like to spend my day and we set up special lunch plans. Valerie organises her travel plans to be with me. When my birthday arrives, I have lots of cards, flowers and gifts from my friends. I feel surrounded by their love. Michael buys me a card and a gift as usual but otherwise does not plan anything special or different.

On this one day, this one significant day, I really want him to take the initiative to care for, nurture and show his love for me in a special, unexpected, romantic way and he doesn't. I feel so exhausted. I am still jet-lagged and shell-shocked. One minute I am with Valerie at my mum's funeral in Bolton and the next I am with her at my 40th birthday in Hong Kong.

I know how Michael loves me—I really know this with all my heart, just as I know how he is fighting constantly for his life and to be with us. This knowledge, however, does not detract from the pain I feel in this moment. These past years have been so hard; I have given so much. At this point, everything becomes too much and a part of me suddenly cries out, "What about me?"

The pain and anger that I feel on this day runs so deep that I spend much of my 40th birthday with Valerie and my other girlfriends feeling very upset. I have not let my feelings of despair, pain and frustration out in this way before. I feel them acutely.

As for Michael, he becomes deeply and genuinely upset when he sees how I feel. He thinks that I have organised what I want for my birthday with my friends and with Valerie's visit. Why wouldn't he? I organise so much in our family life—this is my role. He hasn't really thought that I would desire something more and I haven't told him this, as I want the initiative to come from him. We have a communication breakdown, in the same way that other people do in long-term relationships and marriages, yet with all the additional pressures on us, this one really hurts.

In this book, I am opening up discussion on one of life's taboo subjects— death and dying—and now here I open up another. Perhaps sex is less taboo? It's still a very difficult topic, which I raise in the very sincere hope that I am not alone as someone supporting a partner with a terminal illness and struggling with this issue. I really hope to discuss and learn about this with others. I certainly know that I am not alone in facing a midlife crisis and that neither sex nor death is a topic that we necessarily talk about openly in different societies and cultures. So here goes…

This unexpected eruption of emotion on my 40th birthday abruptly awakens me to the awareness of just how much I've been suppressing my own sensual, sexual and romantic needs in fulfilling my purpose to support Michael and Diana. I've become a mother, I've established a successful career in Hong Kong, I work long hours, I've set up in business, I've become a caregiver and a strong patient advocate, yet somewhere along the way I've lost connection with being Michael's lover. Where have those carefree days of passion gone that I shared with him earlier in our relationship? They are now a distant, faint memory. I feel their loss and the loss of my youth. I think back to earlier relationships with two other long-term lovers in my life, where spending time in bed together was a main focus for our relationships—back then we didn't have any other real responsibilities apart from as lovers and friends. How different life is now.

Knowledge of my unmet desires now stares me in the face, making a stand, demanding to be heard. I'm crying out for attention. Obviously Michael has been getting most of the support and attention over the last few years and, of course, he desperately needs it. He is critically ill; I am not. I have been happy to give this. Yet this imbalance takes a toll, exacerbated somehow by the death of my mum.

The pain of this experience takes time to subside. Michael feels very sorry. I regret my outburst and wish that I had handled things differently before all the emotions boiled over in this way. We gradually talk our way through this experience and it becomes a starting point for change.

As the months pass, Michael and I carve out more time for ourselves and this does help, until he takes on a work project in the UK. He feels very excited by this opportunity, which offers him new professional challenges, and, at first, I am happy to support him as I have with all his other projects. Once he leaves Hong Kong my feelings start to change. I start to question what the point of all this hard work is if we are not even together in person anymore. As long as we remain physically close, I feel that I can handle challenges in our sex life and am willing to work on these.

Years before this, Michael and I attended a course called the Practical Application of Intimate Relationship Skills (PAIRS) as part of my psychotherapy training. I remember a comment made there that marriage is sustained by three pillars: love, friendship and sex. If two of the three are strong, a marriage can usually be sustained. When only one pillar is left standing, a marriage is likely to fail. In our case, the love and friendship pillars are not only strong, they are held in rock-hard cement, a foundation that has only grown stronger over the years. These two pillars are totally and completely unshakeable. Not even a tornado could ever knock those down. It is the third, sex aken a blow.

Sex has always been an integral part of our marriage yet the spontaneity, passion and excitement of sex are harder to retain once Michael becomes terminally ill. There are several contributing factors to this, I believe. As my roles and responsibilities increase I find it harder to engage with feelings of wild sexual abandon. At times, sex is physically difficult, especially after Michael undergoes so many different surgical interventions. In addition, we are both often exhausted and so the very last thing we feel like after a long hard day is sex!

So it is that I find myself in a midlife crisis, with strong emotional waves dashing me against sharp and painful rocks. I mostly talk with Karen and Valerie about my feelings. Karen became my friend at the age of thirteen when she entered my secondary school in Bolton. Karen and Valerie have been with me through my teenage years, my twenties and my thirties. They have seen all of my relationships with men and there is nothing that I do not feel comfortable to talk with them about. I just feel so happy that they are still in my life now.

I feel guilty even having feelings of unhappiness when Michael is critically ill. Yet ultimately being honest with myself, understanding my feelings, and then being open and honest with Michael is what helps us successfully find a path forward together through this painful midlife transition, while remaining faithful to each and every one of our wedding vows.

After confiding in my friends, I speak openly with Michael about my feelings. I have to say that this, for me, is the absolute low point of our marriage. I really wish that I did not have these feelings of unhappiness at this time in my life, and yet I do—and Michael feels so very sad to know this. I can't bear to see him like this. It cuts me up inside to think that I am adding to his burdens. I make my first specific request of him since his cancer diagnosis: I ask him to please stay in Hong Kong with Diana and me. Michael agrees to do so.

I honestly now believe that there is something much deeper than a midlife crisis alone going on at this time. We have both been living a steady stream of endings and beginnings—Michael's heart surgery, radiation treatment and stomach surgery, and the deaths first of my oncologist friend and then of my mum. Additionally, a couple of months after my mum's death, Joyce, her sister, dies. I was very close to my Aunty Joyce, my godmother, as a child and I return to Bolton for the third time for her funeral. At her funeral, the vicar inadvertently says, "It's nice to see you so soon again." He seeks to take back the words the moment they come out of his mouth yet I know exactly what he means. It is a very sad occasion and it feels surreal to be back in the same crematorium. Yet I do take comfort in seeing the vicar again, being with my sister and my dad, as well as my cousins Gillian and Trevor and their families.

We live on a constant seesaw between life and death.

Being so busy fighting for Michael's life, I don't think much consciously about the fact that he is dying, yet I do gradually start to experience him leaving me. This is hard to explain and I'll do my best to find the words, as I know that this transition is one of the difficulties that we face in our marriage at this time. It is as if, somehow, during these eight years of our marriage and Michael's life, he gradually transitions more from living into dying. I witness this very clearly at the end of his life, yet I now see that it began from the moment that he was diagnosed with cancer.

We are constantly facing his dying and, as such, are constantly engaged both in ending our relationship and in fighting to keep it together. This ending is very evident each time Michael undergoes surgery, of course. Another constantly present ending however, like the 'dandelion', is less easily discernible. We are all living and dying at the same time: those of us who are not terminally ill have more latitude to imagine that death is not close at hand.

Michael asks me to listen to a song that he really wants me to hear. He has asked me to do this before at romantic moments in our life, yet never with such deliberate intent. I take notice immediately, without question. Michael's expression of love for me through this song is deeply moving and I come to play it as my personal dedication at Michael's memorial ceremony.

> Do you realize that everyone you know someday will die?
> And instead of saying all of your goodbyes
> Let them know you realize that life goes fast
>
> The Flaming Lips
> 'Do you Realize??'

Michael's choice of lyrics shows him grappling with the reality of his dying. He loves Diana and me with all the strength that he has. He says with all truth and honesty, "Everything that I do, I do for you." It is also true that he is leaving us and I feel it acutely now. He is saying goodbye. I don't want him to leave yet I feel him leaving. He is gradually less engaged with the demands of the physical world, including those of sexual desire. I experience this loss and want to hold on tight to the security that this brings me.

2004 also brings an opportunity for us to buy the house we are renting in Tong Fuk. In order to afford this we must first re-mortgage our house in the UK. I feel so exhausted by this time that I don't want to face this additional challenge even though I know it is a good idea. Michael insists that this is important, so, in addition to successfully building his side of our business, he takes a lead on all financial negotiations. We buy our home in August 2004 and this affords us a welcome cushion of security.

When we lived in Discovery Bay, we employed a female helper to assist us with housework and Diana's care. We now look for new help. Our friend, Celi, who lives in the village, introduces us to her sister who is looking for work. Jenny, a lovely Filipino woman, starts working full-time with us and quickly settles into our family, living with us in our home.

We really value Jenny's help. Over the years in Hong Kong, my work includes travelling around the Asia-Pacific region to deliver Assessment and Development Centre projects. This involves very hard work over long hours and unwinding together socially in the evenings.

Nevertheless, I enjoy working in different countries, meeting and learning from so many people of various nationalities and cultures. Whilst operating independently, I have a sense of partnership and teamwork with colleagues and clients whom I grow close to as friends. Since establishing our business, I am also more in control of the volume of work. This is the perfect balance for me and I feel so happy and proud of my achievements. Michael's work and relationships with colleagues likewise grow from strength to strength so we both feel proud of each other.

Diana settles easily to life in our village. Being very conscious that she is an only child, I have previously worked hard to ensure she has many opportunities for friendship, and it feels a relief that here I don't need to put so much effort into this: two other girls, Susanne and Tiara, also only children, live just around the corner from us. Diana and the girls quickly become friends, and meet and play with other children at home and on the beach. Life in the village is safe. Watching them grow up together I am reminded of my own childhood growing up with Valerie. Given the multicultural environment in which Diana is growing up, she is exposed to many things that I never was. One of these is the Filipino love of dance and music. The children often dance and sing together, putting on performances for special occasions. In September 2004, Diana moves into Primary 2 with Suzy Lambert as her teacher again. She loves her school.

In October 2004, an MRI of Michael's abdomen is clear: 'No significant interval change when compared with the previous MR scan of 2003. No MR evidence to suggest local tumour recurrence or metastatic disease.'

Over this time, Michael continues to research alternative cancer therapy treatments as he has done since his original diagnosis. Our home office gradually fills with books on diets, and bottles of vitamins and herbal supplements appear around the house. Michael does not leave any stone unturned in his search. I'm not going to write of these alternatives in detail as I don't have the depth of knowledge to do so, yet I do know how important the books that Michael read and the people whom he met were to him.

Sometime during 2004, with all that is going on in our lives, Michael learns the desperate news that his dad has lung cancer. At first this is unclear, as Michael's dad does not tell anyone what is happening during regular hospital visits. Michael and his mother suspect that something is wrong when these visits become more frequent and his dad does not want anyone to go with him.

Michael's father's health worsens until, in November 2005, doctors inform his family that he is dying. Michael returns to Scotland to be with him; we agree it is best that I stay home to manage our business and look after Diana. His mum is pleased to see how well Michael is and he gains considerable comfort from being with his family, especially those who travel across from Ireland. His dad dies on 30th November 2005 of lung cancer, having smoked tobacco all his adult life.

The experience of constant shell shock in our lives continues as if we are living in a war zone and yet we are still standing and living our lives in the same way as others!

Cancer Returns Again
August 2006

Attitude is a little thing that makes a big difference.

Winston Churchill

Through most of the following eighteen months, we live 'normal' lives and work hard. We really settle into our home in Tong Fuk, making friends and integrating into the community. We are happy.

In August 2006, we are relaxing at home one evening, when Michael casually reports that he is feeling pain over his right hip. Neither of us thinks much about this. We let the comment pass.

In September, when Diana is in Primary 4, I help out on her first school camp. I hold deeply fond and precious memories of my many camping experiences while growing up, and helping out in this way reconnects me with all of these, which have lain dormant for what feels like a very long time.

Whilst I have nothing but special memories of my first camping experiences in the North of England, they are also ones that feature a lot of rain, sheltering to keep warm, and cagoules (waterproof jackets)! How different it is for Diana. The children camp in South Lantau alongside Pui O beach. They run and play on a vast, open expanse of sand; swim in the sea; fish with string, bread and safety pins in the stream—and the key challenge is ensuring that they have enough sunscreen on! How things have changed in my life over the past fourty years, yet the warmth of the campfire at night and the company of friends around it remain exactly the same.

This particular camp brings unexpected, indeed unwanted, drama. The children are all in bed, attempting to settle into sleep. I am in a tent with four young girls who, exhausted from over-excitement from the day's activities, have immediately collapsed fast asleep, unlike me! Despite my love of camping, I long for my comfy bed!

As I lie willing myself to sleep, listening to the steady lapping of the waves, I become increasingly aware of raised adult voices. The volume intensifies into what is evidently a fight, one that builds to such a point that I immediately feel the children might be in danger. Having lain with the escalating noise level for some time I am now connected with primal, maternal emotions that drive me to protect the children. Like a tigress, I leap out of my tent ready to fight. It is only later when I see other people looking at me that I notice I am actually wearing pyjamas and wonder what on earth I thought that I was going to do! What chance does logic stand when maternal instincts take over!

The scene in front of me is of a very drunk or drugged man, verbally abusing and physically threatening his girlfriend. In this moment I am ready to do what it takes to protect the children on my own! There is a small group of other men at the scene, one of whom I recognise as Tom, a Primary 6 teacher with whom I have not had much contact. I feel very wary of a couple of the men at the scene and mention my feelings to Tom, who agrees with me. As those present call the police and handle this violent situation, I gradually experience this teacher as someone who is absolutely to be trusted and allow myself to lean on his strength.

By 3 am, I am aware of my vulnerability and, not least, my pyjamas! By 4, I have established enough of a sense of comfort to leave this situation in Tom's hands and return to my tent. I am struck by how often over recent years I have leant on my own strength in traumatic moments and how different this feels: it is like being able to have a brief emotional rest.

Suzy and her husband Jim, both teachers at the same school, are already my friends and, from this camp onwards, Tom also becomes one. In fact, I spend so much time hanging out with the teachers over the years that I start to feel like an additional arm of the teaching team, which is really special and supportive for me. And it is not only the teachers whom I become friends with at this time. I get to know other parents as well and, in particular, I become friends with

Pete and Maureen, Dina, Paul and Rose, and Pete and Michelle, who remain important in my life today.

This period of respite, where I get to enjoy the open air and teamwork of school camp, is indeed a very brief one. In November 2006, a PET scan reveals:

> A solitary hypermetabolic lytic expansile lesion at right iliac bone involving the right acetabulum. Soft tissue with possible central ecrosis associated with this lytic bone lesion is found....
>
> The original tumour bed in the heart and the upper abdomen are disease free.

The cancer has returned again, this time in Michael's pelvis.

The orthopaedic surgeon investigates and offers Michael surgical removal of part of his pelvis, but Michael has been conducting further investigations of his own. He has located a research institute in Australia that provides an alternative therapy treatment called radio-therapy. This is different from radiation treatment.

The radio-therapy treatment is in its experimental stages and Michael's doctors do not support it. Michael, however, simply cannot bear to think that he will continue to live his life with different major body parts being cut away. His doctors help us to ask pertinent questions of the institute, such as "Have they ever had experience of the cancer spreading as a result of the treatment?" They assure us that they have not. Michael decides to go ahead with the alternative therapy treatment and travels to Perth that month. By the time Michael returns home, he is feeling ever-increasing levels of pain. He does not know if this is a good or a bad sign. The institute informs him that there can be increased pain in the healing process. As Michael's pain increases, we book an appointment with the surgeon in early January 2007.

The situation is critical. Whether due to the radio-therapy treatment or not, we have no way of knowing, but Michael's cancer has spread rapidly. Previously, the surgeon had thought that he could do the pelvic surgery in isolation. Now he tells Michael that it is also necessary to amputate his right leg.

Michael has been a recipient of bad news many times, yet I have never ever seen him look so shocked. He stares at me in disbelief: "If I had known that there was a risk of me losing my leg, I would never have gone to Australia." We are both blown away by this news.

This is a major operation called a 'hemipelvectomy', which involves the amputation of half of his right pelvis and his right leg. Surgery has to be as fast as possible, with our facing all the usual additional complexities like needing to obtain his rare blood type through the Red Cross. In preparing Michael for surgery, his leg swells to over twice its normal size in less than a week, to the point where both of us feel absolutely desperate for it to be removed.

Can you imagine how it is to move from the complete shock that you need to have your right leg amputated to the absolute desire for it to be removed—within less than a week?

Preparations for Michael's surgery coincide with Diana's 8th birthday. For the past few years Diana has chosen to spend her birthday in Hong Kong Disneyland and this year is no exception. Determined for her to enjoy her birthday, with support from my friends, I plan her party to take place at Disneyland in the morning and for me to join them in the afternoon and later for dinner and birthday cake. In this way, I can spend time with both Michael and Diana.

I spend the morning of Diana's birthday in the hospital whilst Michael is undergoing all kinds of tests and the doctors are extremely concerned. I cannot bear for him to be going through this again. I don't want to leave his side. I feel absolutely exhausted as I make my way alone to Disneyland. Upon arrival, the completely surreal juxtaposition between the intensity of the hospital and the fantasy world of Disney is incredibly difficult to bear. To cap it all, the first thing that I have to cope with on arrival is the fact that my credit card is lost. I can't stand it. I want to scream. Instead, I sit on a carousel horse and go around in circles with tears streaming down my face. After a short while, I go and join the children who are having so much fun.

At this time, Michael and I feel the full weight of support from our village community behind us. Friends such as Boz, Vandra and Caroline make time after work to visit Michael. In fact, so many of our good friends and neighbours are with us at the hospital before Michael goes in for surgery that the ward is packed and we are not at all popular with the nursing staff, especially when the guys decide to play cards, which they are stopped from doing! Our friends Cheryl and Ed also invite the pastor from their church to say prayers with Michael.

The surgery is prepared, and once again it is life-threatening.

Diana, now eight years old, and I say goodbye to Michael for the third time.

Whilst Michael is in surgery, about fifteen female friends and various children join Diana and me at 'Snoopy World' in Shatin. Many of our closest friends are with us and this makes it an incredibly special way to spend such an afternoon. We laugh and talk over lunch and the children enjoy the rides. Both of us feel loved and held. Incredibly, I hold positive memories of the afternoon now, even given the acutely painful context.

Once again, Michael survives. He is, however, so ill: he is jet-lagged, he is grieving the loss of his father, and he has been through so very much that none of us expects him to survive this major surgery.

We all say hello again for the third time.

I immediately phone Michael's mum in the UK to let her know the good news. She draws on the support of her family and her church.

I'd like to quote from two of our friends in their later sharing about this particular moment:

> The day that Michael had his leg amputated, Barbara and I were able to be at the hospital. Barbara was in the room with Diana and Jenny when Sandra was called down to the ICU after the operation and Sandra asked if I could go with her. I went down with her to the ICU. Bear in mind that we are talking about maybe an hour and 45 minutes after the operation—a colossal operation and this is an amazing example of strength.
>
> As we walked into the ICU—an eight-bed, frantically active ICU—Michael was in the bed just inside the door on the right. He was lying there, very very pale, very very weak, but he was lying there, holding his oxygen mask off with his left hand and instructing the nurse at the foot of the bed as to exactly where he wanted a particular piece of equipment: "A wee bit to the right..."
>
> Paddy

I remember the night that I went up into the ICU just after he had had his leg amputated and spent some time with him by myself and the first thing that he said to me was, "Oh, how are you Boz?"

Here he was, he'd just come out from under the anaesthetic, I mean within a couple of hours, most of his entire right side almost was gone from below the hip, including the hip, and he asked me how I was. I've got an incredible memory of how strong he was and his persistence—he was completely persistent.

One day I had a problem sending out some faxes on my computer and Michael had just arrived home [from hospital after the operation] and I asked if I could send him a fax to see if it came through on his fax machine and he said, "Sure".

The fax didn't come through properly, so he said, "Come over and we'll fix it up."

So I went over to his and Sandra's place and we were sitting down together trying to sort this problem out and nothing was too difficult for him.

Even my problem, a technical problem, he was just completely prepared in the face of what he was feeling to actually get down and solve that problem. To me, that's an example of a human being that can really put the needs of others above his own needs, no matter what he is feeling at the time.

Boz

Our friends Jörg and Winnie host a celebration party in their garden. The campfire is lit and all of our friends from the village are with me whilst Michael is at the hospital with an old friend. The community in Tong Fuk is unlike any other that I have experienced in my life. It is a small, local, Hong Kong Chinese village with people of many different nationalities, cultures and religious backgrounds living in it. One of our regular and favourite activities is to meet outside to share food and drink. These parties, often impromptu, are always so relaxed, and the wide selection of homemade food prepared with love for minimal cost is always amazing and internationally inspired: Chinese, Thai, Filipino, Australian, German, South African, New Zealand, British and Argentinean.

I have had a song playing in my head for the past week. Our friends Tom and Nong's son, Daniel, kindly records the song for me onto a memory stick. We hook up a CD player in Jörg and Winnie's garden. Then we play the song and sing Gerry & The Pacemakers' rousing chorus down the phone to Michael:

Walk on, walk on, with hope in your heart
And you'll never walk alone.

Rodgers & Hammerstein
'You'll Never Walk Alone'

As we sing to Michael down the telephone, we are celebrating the inspiration of life. We do not know that this is also one of the last moments where Michael is able to deeply feel and cherish the love, care and concern of his local community. In some ways, we don't need to know, yet, in others, I also look back now and think how valuable it is to hold the knowledge that each moment in life is both part of our living and also part of our dying.

Living with Disability
January 2007

If you're going through hell, keep going.

Winston Churchill

We prepare for Michael's homecoming following the amputation of his leg.

Michael never just wanted to know what; he insisted on knowing why and how. Barbara and I witnessed this with Sandra and him in great detail as Michael's medical condition developed and changed and indeed became ever-increasingly worse. At no time did Michael and Sandra stop searching; they met and made phone calls with friends, with complete strangers, looking for information about matters medical, medicinal and surgical to help them understand what was going on, what was on hand and how to deal with what must be, to such a degree that I know very well that they won a very significant amount of respect from the very senior people whom they were dealing with at the Prince of Wales Hospital.

In short, Michael was an immensely strong and courageous person throughout this dreadful business. I have some particular illustrations. Very shortly after the amputation of Michael's leg, Terry, I remember, Boz and some other guys were there. We were standing around thinking how the devil we could adapt the surroundings of Sandra and Michael's house—different layers of walkways, the steps and so on and so forth—to accommodate the inevitable wheelchair. And, we had grand plans for sweeping ramps and various devices. As soon as Michael got wind of this, he said, "Stop. None of that! Don't adapt the environment to me. I shall adapt to the environment!" And in no time at all, he had got it hacked. Amazing!

Paddy

And so it is that Michael returns home. The day after, we attend Diana's primary school sports day to encourage her as a family. With support from us all, Michael adapts very quickly to his disability and to his environment. In the early stages, Michael is not yet able to walk upstairs. Our friends bring a white plastic sun-lounger into the living room and, with the help of wooden pallets, try to adjust it to the right height for Michael to be able to get onto it.

Terry recalls:

> The most important thought in my mind, as a friend, was to be able to help someone and to be there if needed for both the hard discussions and the day-to-day talk. With the house it was important not to make Michael feel like an invalid, which I hope did not happen.
>
> Michael always seemed so direct and positive about what he wanted. I recall popping around one evening when there was a crowd in your living room. Michael was home; he needed to get set up. I screw-fixed the bed to the wooden pallets, me on my knees with the screwdriver, Michael above me with directions for alignment and height adjustment. Many such occasions spring to mind.

Soon Michael is walking up two flights of stairs to our bedroom rather than having us rearrange our home for him to sleep downstairs. We also continue with our social life: indeed friends are often at our home. Michael walks to The Gallery on crutches, refusing the use of a wheelchair.

In addition to learning to live with Michael's disability, there is something else deeply concerning in our minds. During the preparations for the loss of half of Michael's pelvis and his leg, some activity showed up in the scans of his heart. It looks like there might be cancerous activity in the primary site of his original tumour, which would mean that the amputation of his leg had been in vain.

During this time, we decide to bring Jenny's husband, Dwight, from the Philippines to employ him as well. Michael is heavy to lift and the demands on Jenny and me have become too great. We really need an extra pair of male hands. It is also at this time that people who know us—yet not so well—start to realise and to comment on just how ill Michael is. One restaurant where we like to relax in South

Lantau is called The Stoep. I gradually come to know the manager, Mei, and her staff, who are quite shocked to see Michael soon after the loss of his leg. He has also by now lost more and more weight due in part to various diets that he has tried, including a complete fast that he undertook for several weeks determined to rid all cancer cells from his body.

About one month after the hemipelvectomy, we celebrate the attainment of our permanent residency status in Hong Kong. For us this is a very big deal. Each year since we established our business we have had to submit financial accounts and paperwork to prove to the Hong Kong government that we have the right to remain living here. We have met all stipulations, including the employment of locals and renting of an office, as well as showing steady financial growth. Each year, in addition to living with the constant uncertainties of Michael's health, we have never known whether or not we might be thrown out of the country if we have a bad business year, which has been a pretty significant motivator for working very hard! To remove such a considerable layer of uncertainty from under our feet really is an incredible relief and most definitely a moment to celebrate.

We decide to visit the same restaurant that Harold took us to on our very first trip to Hong Kong together for one the look-see visits, when Michael was deciding whether or not to join his company. We feel very emotional being there, reminiscing over how much our lives have changed since then. Thinking back to dreams that we shared when we arrived and about the direction that life has taken tinges our nostalgia with a sense of loss.

It is the middle of the afternoon when we leave. The restaurant steps are steep. Michael loses his balance and falls. Immediately, people rush to our aid and he is soon on his feet again, although having lost confidence. My heart sinks in this moment. I want to rest in our celebration, to believe this is a positive changing point in our lives yet, honestly, in my heart of hearts, I have a terrible instinct that something is very wrong and I no longer trust that we will be able to continue sharing our life paths and dreams together.

Michael's heart surgeon, after careful deliberation, offers him the option of a second heart surgery. By this stage in our lives, the surgeon has become a friend and he describes himself as being like a brother to Michael.

Michael is clear. He has come this far. If he doesn't get rid of the cancer from his heart then he has absolutely no chance of survival. The odds are all stacked against him.

We don't see the surgeon for several days before Michael's surgery. Later he explains to me how the only way that he can do this particularly complex surgery—given Michael's physical state—is by emotionally distancing himself from Michael.

I follow Michael's bed down to the doors of the surgery until I can walk no further. I say "I love you" and "I'll see you soon." We kiss goodbye.

This is now the fourth time that Diana and I have said goodbye to Michael as he enters his fourth major surgery and second heart operation.

I have never, ever seen this surgeon look as completely and utterly exhausted as he is when Michael's surgery is over. It is a success. Michael recovers.

Diana and I, with family and friends, welcome Michael back to us for the fourth time. Our lives are becoming increasingly different from 'normal'.

With his incredible strength and will power, Michael returns home after a short time in hospital. I want everything to be comfortable now and long for Michael's complete recovery. As usual, Michael rests for what seems to me like an incredibly brief period of time and then returns to being focused and motivated by his work.

I notice that his mental activity is different. I can't quite put my finger on what it is but know in my heart that something is wrong. My instincts remain attuned to the same mood that I felt when Michael fell after our lunch in Central. I feel frightened when I listen to them, as if we are now fighting a losing battle. Everything, including Michael's return to work, is moving too fast for me.

Sadly, my instincts prove correct again. A couple of months later, Michael complains of pain in his buttock. All the nerves and sinews in my body tense up involuntarily as I hear his words and as I long so much to ignore them. I feel so frightened that I can hardly bear to listen.

I voice the unthinkable: "Perhaps your cancer is back?"

Michael replies, "It can't be because the margins from the amputation of my leg were clear."

Whatever our thoughts and feelings, we both know from bitter experience that we cannot afford to deny this pain—time is, once again, not our friend.

On 6th August 2007, we receive the latest of all the many MRI reports that we have read over the years, confirming our worst nightmare:

> IMPRESSION:
> Multiple masses at right pelvis. In view of history, these are
> likely metastasis lesions.

Anyone who has ever read these kinds of medical reports will understand the deep-seated feelings of terror, dread, nausea, pain and rage that immediately attack the gut on reading these stark, factual words. This is the worst possible news.

One reason Michael is still alive after eight years is that we have learned to find ways to keep tuned into our heads as well as our hearts and feelings during times of acute stress. An ambitious, some might say unrealistic, attitude, yet Michael's life has consistently depended on close judgment calls.

The words of Rudyard Kipling's 'If' come to mind:

> If you can force your heart and nerve and sinew
> To serve your turn long after they are gone,
> And so hold on when there is nothing in you
> Except the Will which says to them: 'Hold on!'

Reading the medical report, we both feel sheer panic—where on earth can we go next? There isn't much of Michael's body left that hasn't been cut away or treated.

We lean on the constant, unswerving support of our friends and we take action, with me phoning, writing, speaking to everyone whom we can think of out of sheer desperation to find a cure, an answer, a miracle, anything that can simply help us to change the reality that we are facing.

Just before Michael is admitted back into hospital, our good friends Jilly and Ed invite us for the most wonderfully long, leisurely Sunday breakfast with eggs frying on the barbecue in the sunshine. Jilly almost decides not to invite us as she feels concerned that their house is in a mess because they are having refurbishment work done. Thankfully she invites us anyway, as this turns out to be the last social event that Michael attends in his home village in South Lantau.

Michael's oncologists, who have been at our side for many years enabling Michael to stay alive, now face us again, this time telling us that there are no more radiation or chemotherapy drugs that can help Michael. We both feel a door close in front of us, and we rail against it with all our shared might.

Michael's orthopaedic surgeon then stands again at the foot of the bed also telling us there is nothing more that he can do. Michael honestly voices to him the stark reality of his experience: "The cancer is eating me alive from the inside. Help me."

I feel totally and utterly helpless, desperate. The orthopaedic surgeon offers to look again at the scans of Michael's pelvis.

I phone Michael's heart surgeon who no longer works at the Prince of Wales Hospital, yet we have come to trust and lean on him so much over the years that we want him with us again. As always, he returns my call.

He offers to speak with colleagues in Switzerland whom he knows have been using drug regimes for the treatment of leiomyosarcoma, which they refer to as 'off label use therapy'. We have no idea what these terms mean.

The oncologist tells us that the drugs are expensive and are only available on a case-by-case basis in Hong Kong.

"How much more deserving can Michael be than anyone else in the world," I argue, "given that he has been successfully fighting this disease for eight years? Surely, if anyone deserves not to be deserted now, then it is him. Don't let the cost of the drugs be a hurdle. Please see if you can get them for us. Let us know the cost and we will take whatever action we can to get the money."

The oncologist agrees to consult his colleagues and those in Switzerland.

One of the many important lessons that we have learned over the years is the need for a patient advocate, someone to stand by the side of the patient, arguing his case, asking questions, researching information. We have found this to be a full-time job!

Another important lesson we have learned is that the only person who holds 100% of the overview of the whole treatment programme is the patient, in our case, Michael. I come second with perhaps 75% of the overall picture though many times, despite my best efforts, I simply cannot retain the same level of detailed information as Michael. Because so many medical practitioners and specialists are involved in different aspects of patient care, especially in Michael's case where his condition is so rare, no single one comes close to this same view, although some are closer than others. The medical practitioner with the widest overview in our case is Michael's oncologist, whom we meet on a regular basis and who acts as a link with other doctors.

We have learned how vital it is for us to take ownership of Michael's care: a very different perspective from the one that we were both raised with, of putting ourselves into the hands of doctors who have 'right' answers. Over time we have adopted a model more of partnership than dependency. We have come to believe that this approach has directly helped Michael to live longer than anyone else with this condition.

Respect for varying opinions is also inherent in the Hong Kong government healthcare system, which differs in this regard from the private system, I believe. In government healthcare, doctors work in teams to support the patient, vociferously arguing, sometimes with vastly different perspectives and views amongst them. We develop inherent respect for the integrity of this system and now fear those where the doctors are concerned to offer only one 'right' answer.

Michael's orthopaedic surgeon returns, talking through the films with us in detail. With the assistance of a specialist team, he is prepared to go into Michael's pelvis to remove the tumour. The risks are high, yet he offers to get the team together the following week if Michael wants to. The message is clear: a quick decision is imperative. As he later writes:

Michael is a known patient suffering from Metastatic Leiomyosarcoma of the heart. He had a hindquarter amputation in January 2007 for locally advanced metastatic lesion in the right pelvi-acetabular region.

Following a brief interval in which Michael was in remission, the tumour recurred in the soft tissue around the pelvic floor and around the left sacral ala. The tumour was closely adherent to the rectum and the bladder.

A PET-CT done showed the presence of metastatic tumour in the pelvis and metastatic tumour in the right lung.

The treatment plan for Michael's recurrent disease was predicted on:

a) Complete resection of the pelvic tumour followed by

b) Suitable adjuvant therapy—such as radiation for the tumour bed and

c) Possible systemic therapy for pulmonary lesions.

The frequency with which Michael has undergone major surgery belittles not only the severity of the risks but also the multiplicity of problems and difficulties that he faces each time. Although we are now strangely familiar with life-and-death decisions, we also know this one is underpinned by more desperation than others. We face another high-risk surgery or await drugs that we might or might not be able to get hold of.

Michael is again painfully honest with me: "I am terrified of knowing that the cancer is eating me from inside. I've fought this far. I have to do anything possible to get this cancer out of me. I don't just want to wait to die." The decision is made. Michael opts for surgery. Once more, I don't expect Michael to survive—how can he? How can one man survive so much?

Even Diana, at eight years old, knows how critically ill her daddy is as we kiss him goodbye for the fifth time.

The surgeon later writes:

> On 16th August 2007, Michael underwent pelvic surgery. A bowel diversion was done anticipating the likelihood of possible rectal involvement and obstruction. A laparoscopic assisted colostomy was performed.

Pacing familiar hospital corridors with Paddy once again at my side, as he was for Michael's recent heart surgery, I am very concerned that the surgery should have finished a long time ago. Thankfully, Paddy has the kind of inner strength that I can really lean on. He and Barbara have witnessed the deaths of many young pilots when Paddy worked in the military air force and they supported their widows. Without question, they remain by our sides, like close family, lending unswerving support. Words will never ever be enough to thank them.

As expatriates, we all face the particular challenges of living far away from our own families. This alone does not provide a reason for others to step in and unselfishly help. Yet in facing all the difficulties that we have, we consistently experience a side of Hong Kong in which members of our community not only care deeply, but also work tirelessly alongside us to lend support.

My instincts are correct as ever in telling me that something is wrong. For the first time in eight years, the surgeon faces me with bad news. I hear some words:

"The surgery didn't go as planned."

"The cancer was more widespread than we saw on the scans."

"We stayed in as long as possible, then we had to get out because Michael lost a lot of blood so we had to do transfusions and finish the surgery early."

"We weren't able to remove all of the cancer."

"The cancer is much worse than we have expected; it is in his veins and his lungs so it is now travelling through his whole system."

As I struggle to hear or make meaning of the surgeon's words, nurses push Michael out of the theatre on a bed. His body is swollen like a large bloated balloon, almost unrecognisable as him. I start to follow the bed as if in a dream.

I say hello again to Michael for the fifth time in eight years; for the first time, he is not in a position to say hello back to me.

As the surgeon later writes:

> The pelvis tumour was resected. We were unable to attain wide margins as the tumour could not be easily separated from the bladder and part of the tumour was resected with intra-lesional margins.
>
> Michael's post operative recovery was hampered by his deteriorating lung function. This is most likely the result of his progressive disease in the lung.
>
> CT of the thorax has shown progressive lesions in both the right and left lung. He has significant pleural effusion on both sides and significant fibrosis of the lung parenchyma especially on the right side.
>
> At present, Michael's condition is stable. He continues to have respiratory distress although his vital signs and saturation have been maintained satisfactorily.
>
> It is our view that Michael's condition is pre-terminal and our team does not think any further oncologic or surgical treatment is likely to be effective.

In Intensive Care
August 2007

If children have the ability to ignore all odds and percentages, then maybe we can all learn from them. When you think about it, what other choice is there but to hope? We have two options, medically and emotionally: give up, or fight like hell.

Lance Armstrong

And so begins my vigil in the ICU...

I find the ICU to be a unique and strangely addictive world—one in which I find myself surrounded by doctors and families handling knife-edge, life-and-death decisions moment to moment—not every few years or every few months, as I had become familiar with since Michael's diagnosis. This reality focuses the mind. As I sit by Michael's bed, patients of all ages, shapes and sizes are wheeled in and out of adjacent beds attached to various tubes and machines. I'm not experiencing detachment from my own pain as such, yet I am gaining a new-found sense of awareness and even fascination for the workings of ICU beyond the individual experience of pain suffered by Michael and me.

Michael's heart surgeon comes by to visit Michael as a friend on his first evening out of surgery. Looking back, I think that this is the last time that he sees Michael alive. His parting words echo in my ears: "I have never seen a man's body so swollen. I don't know how they will bring the swelling down."

As soon as I hear his words, I know what we are dealing with. At this time, Diana is with my friend Sally and her family, who have welcomed us into their home, a short drive away from the hospital in Shatin on the way to Sai Kung. Sally is an actress whom I have come to know through working on a corporate project together. A few years earlier we met unexpectedly at the airport when she was travelling home for the funeral of one of her parents. Now, she welcomes us without question into her home and simply gives me a key. Once again, how do I begin to say thank you?

Sai Kung is a beautiful area of Hong Kong with large country parks and spectacular scenery, but I have no time for enjoying it. My only goal is to sleep and to be with Diana. In the night, I receive an emergency call from the hospital—they don't expect Michael to live. Sally and her husband, Paul, immediately bundle Diana into bed with them, keeping her safe and warm as I catch a cab.

Michael is delirious. He doesn't recognise me. He is attached to machines and monitoring equipment. The head of the ICU asks if we have made decisions about whether or not to attach Michael to a life support system should the need arise. We have discussed every aspect of Michael's living, dying and treatment to date, yet never even considered this question. I am unprepared. I don't know what to do.

Several times, I am asked to leave the room as his monitors bleep and blink. Paddy has driven across to Shatin again to be with me. In the dark corridor in the middle of the night we start to plan how we will make arrangements to fly Michael's body home to Scotland and we begin to make phone calls. Paddy apologises in a very British way for the fact that he has already started to conduct investigations into how to organise the repatriation of Michael's body. I am deeply grateful to him.

Michael survives the night. Over the coming day, he begins to settle and his swelling starts to reduce. He has brief moments where he is lucid and can recognise me. I am called into a meeting with the doctors.

Surrounding me in the room are most of the key medical players in Michael's life at this time: the oncologist, the orthopaedic surgeon and the Head of the ICU. Each person in turn faces me and tells me that Michael will die, that there is nothing more that they can do to help him. It is impossible to find the words to describe how acutely painful this experience is for me.

It is as if all the physicians who have enabled Michael to live in the past are now switching out the lights of life one at a time. I feel all hope extinguished with every word. I am alone in the dark. I feel as if I have died. It is hard to speak. I stare at the faces of each of the doctors, trying to hold onto my pride. Tears fill my eyes, rolling down my face.

The doctors tell me that I have to make a decision whether or not I want them to put Michael onto a life support machine if and when we face that moment.

A surge of anger flares up within me: "Michael and I have made all decisions together so far. If there is anything that he deserves now, it is to be involved in this decision. I will make it only if I absolutely have to."

I fall out of the room into my friend Sally, who has just walked through the doors of ICU. We are ushered into a side room where I sob my heart out, falling gratefully into her supportive arms.

The doctors agree that my request to consult Michael is fair, telling me that I should call them if I see a time when I think that Michael is lucid enough to make this decision. That time arises the next day. The doctors respond immediately to my call to Michael's bedside as I speak with him, "Michael, there is one question that we have never discussed. If we face a time when the doctors need to decide whether to put you onto a life support machine, what would you like to do?"

Michael responds with clarity, "I only want to do it if it will give me six months or more of life."

Later, the orthopaedic surgeon and the head of ICU explain to me just how incredible it is that a man as critically ill as Michael could give a crystal-clear answer, not to a simple question like "What is your name?" but to a sophisticated, high-level, life-and-death decision. They respect my choice and respect Michael's. He makes it; we witness it. His answer is the same as doctors hear from the majority of patients facing this awful decision.

I speak with Michael privately, before the doctors meet him, about what they are saying. I want him to hear this first from me. I desperately want him to feel more prepared than I was. I know I can't rescue him but would give anything in the world to do so. I hold his hand firmly. I want him to feel every ounce of my presence, to know I am with him, beside him, strong. I love him.

Later, I watch as these doctors, who have each provided him with life support for so many years, one by one, say goodbye to Michael, to tell him that there is no more that they can do and to shake his hand. Michael listens. Tears fall down his cheeks—and he is not a man who cries.

Then he rallies strength, yet again, as I have seen him do so many times before. Michael looks the oncologist straight in the eye and firmly requests that he supports him in finding out more information on the drug regime in use in Switzerland. The mutual respect in this moment is tangible. The oncologist gives Michael, now a man firmly condemned to death, his promise and assurance on this. In the midst of nothing but darkness, there is a door that is ajar, offering a slight glimmer of light and hope that means the world to us.

When All Hope is Gone
August 2007 cont.

Once upon a time there was light in my life
But now there's only love in the dark

Bonnie Tyler
'Total Eclipse of the Heart'

We now experience life at a deep turning point. The focus of Michael's care now is to manage his dying so Michael is removed from ICU where the focus is on saving lives. I feel surprised when Michael's orthopaedic surgeon tells me, "Surely you knew that my surgery was palliative care?"

> Palliative care is an approach that improves the quality of life of patients and their families facing the problem associated with life-threatening illness, through the prevention and relief of suffering by means of early identification and impeccable assessment and treatment of pain and other problems, physical, psychosocial and spiritual.
>
> The World Health Organisation

I recognise that labelling this transition can have value, but for us at this point, it sounds like another door slamming death into our face. I think of palliative care as having negative connotations, administered when someone is dying. We still refuse to allow this situation to drain us of all the hope that has sustained us so far. Looking back at the early medical reports, they actually refer to Michael's treatment as palliative care. For example, on 2nd March 2000, an oncologist wrote: 'He is now under my care, receiving palliative radiotherapy to the whole heart.'

The words of a song flow into my mind as I write. It is a song that my friend and neighbour Elize introduces me to, called 'Dante's Prayer' by Loreena McKennitt. The words and music of the song are like a form of prayer. I believe that I recall them now as they soothe the pain of my memories in sharing this part of my life journey with you:

> When the dawn seemed forever lost
> You showed me your love in the light of the stars

And so a dual-fold process opens up: we prepare for Michael's dying whilst not losing hope for his living. He has beaten the odds by surviving ICU, hasn't he? We have some more time, don't we? 'Hope' is such a small word, with such a powerful impact. This simple noun is defined in *Webster's Dictionary* as 'desire accompanied with expectation of obtaining what is desired or belief that it is obtainable'.

Michael tells me that there is one alternative therapy cure that he has not tried, which is based on the digestion of B17 vitamins. We check whether taking these vitamins can cause Michael any harm. It seems not. I then set about what turns out to be my final project of hope and, with the unerring support of my friends, give it my all.

Elize and other friends search health shops and learn that B17 vitamins are not on sale in Hong Kong. I call an old friend, Joanne, in South Africa and ask her to look. I e-mail Annie and Steve in Australia and Caroline in the UK. I have a pencil-drawn spreadsheet with me in the hospital and I gather the data that we all collect. We find them on sale through a website in Mexico and place the order online. I then speak with friends who work as pilots and aircrew. Through incredible worldwide coordination, we are able to have them delivered to the USA where our friend Julia picks them up and brings them home to Tong Fuk Village. I keep Michael informed of every step of this journey.

To be honest, at this stage, I don't believe that the B17 vitamins can help him, yet I do absolutely believe in the power of hope and I am determined that Michael will continue to have access to hope amongst all the other emotions that he has. I am not letting go until I absolutely have to, nor are any of our friends—holding onto hope when all seems lost is now a global team effort.

While we search for vitamins, Michael's oncologist introduces us to a new doctor, a woman from their palliative team, who will now be in charge of Michael's care. She begins to talk about options in choosing where Michael will die. There are some specialist hospices in Hong Kong, which support patients with 'end of life' care. My friend, Pamela, drives us with another friend to visit one south of Hong Kong Island. It is a beautiful, tranquil place with alternative therapies and evident care for the patients.

Yet, for me, this visit is very shocking, especially when they walk me through the dying process, showing me a room especially prepared for dying patients. The room is made up to look like a bedroom in a house in order to help patients feel more restful. The ICU and the hospice environments are complete and utter polar opposites. One is frantic, noisy and fast-paced, focused moment to moment on saving lives. The other is extremely quiet and prepares people for certain death. I am not ready for this. Please... not yet...

Michael's oncologist is genuinely sorry that I face such a shock on visiting the hospice, understanding, to my great relief, exactly why I feel this way, given the contrast to the frenzy of ICU where I have been for the past ten days. I am so grateful for his empathy and evident concern.

Again with friends, we visit another hospice closer to, and linked with, the Prince of Wales Hospital. This second experience is easier for me and I can really value the special care and support that hospices are able to offer. I still don't know if these are right for us at this time.

The doctors then intervene. Having spoken with both hospices, they are now clear that these do not have the medical facilities to support someone who has just experienced all the surgeries that Michael has. He needs the kind of specialist medical care that they can only provide in the hospital and we might not have time to move him.

Michael asks if he can go home. Our close friend and neighbour, Sue, has already been helping us to see if there might be any medical and nursing support for this, even for him to just go home for one day.

The final outcome is, sadly, that Michael never comes home with us again.

Finding Ceci
August 2007 cont.

It's not easy to live every moment wholly aware of death. It's like trying to stare the sun in the face: you can stand only so much of it. Because we cannot live frozen in fear, we generate methods to soften death's terror. We project ourselves into the future through our children; we grow rich, famous, ever larger; we develop compulsive protective rituals; or we embrace an impregnable belief in an ultimate rescuer.

Irvin D. Yalom
Staring at the Sun: Overcoming the Dread of Death

When my friend Sue searches the Internet to see if it is possible to find the support of Macmillan nurses for Michael to die at home, she is led to papers written by Professor Cecilia L.W. Chan, Ph.D., Department of Social Work and Social Administration at the University of Hong Kong. Sue is deeply moved by a conversation with Professor Chan (Ceci) and she urges me to speak with Ceci myself.

Ceci returns my call as I travel home from the hospital across the mountain. Her words are like a gentle stream of fresh water slowly washing over me, soothing and healing. She explains the work of her team at the Centre for Behavioral Health in supporting families and communities with death and dying.

She says, "The experience that you are going through right now is like a non-stop emotional roller-coaster. It is physically, emotionally, and spiritually demanding and exhausting."

She understands what I am going through! The process of dying is familiar to her and, even more than this, I feel the depth of her empathy. She knows what she is talking about and she cares. I am seen and heard by Ceci. In her recognition of my experience, I know others have felt these feelings before me and will do so after me. I am not alone. I feel relief.

There is one key message I take away from this conversation—and it is a complete paradigm shift: "This time that you have together now, these are the last precious moments that you will share together as a family," Ceci explains.

Her words focus my mind. In the midst of all the anguish, pain, suffering and medical dramas, I only experience these times as the exact opposite to precious. I begin to feel a new sense of purpose and direction. I focus on living these last moments with Michael. I focus more on living than dying.

Ceci then asks, "How do you want to spend these last precious moments together?"

In so doing, she gives me a new conceptual focus and I begin to engage with a different, more positive energy. I don't have an answer for Ceci, yet, as I look out over the mountains and down to the sea, I start to imagine how we might spend our precious time together. I know now that none of us knows which precious moments will be our last. This is a lesson in living.

* * *

Again the words and music of Loreena McKennitt's 'Dante's Prayer' flow into my mind as I write:

> Though we share this humble path, alone
> How fragile is the heart

* * *

I schedule an appointment with Ceci a few days before Michael's death. I have agreed to film all my meetings with Ceci so that we can later produce teaching videos from which others can benefit and learn. I switch off my mobile phone for the duration of the filming. When I switch it back on again there are several urgent messages from the hospital. They are losing Michael and tell me to return as quickly as possible. Diana is with me. We drop everything and rush back.

Ceci says, "Look after your husband and care for him as if he was pregnant, as he looked after you when you were pregnant. Take him his favourite foods, drinks and music."

I remember how Michael reaches out to me in ICU after all the doctors told him that they could no longer help: "We must drink that special bottle of red wine that we have been saving."

* * *

We have told our friends before of one wedding anniversary we celebrate in a renowned hotel in Hong Kong. Michael sees a bottle of red wine, Nuits Saint Georges, on the menu: the same brand as the first bottle of wine that he ever bought in his life. He hesitates to buy it, as the price is so high, then decides to go ahead anyway. We enjoy the wine and relax over dinner.

When the bill arrives, Michael is taken aback and calls the waiter back to explain that the wine costs double what he was expecting. The waiter, very professionally and politely, returns to our table with the menu and shows Michael that the price he actually saw was for the half bottle. I cannot stop laughing. The moment is one of those special ones never to be forgotten by either of us, especially Michael, who with his strong working-class Scottish roots, had found the whole experience somewhat challenging!

A few years later, I buy another bottle of Nuits Saint Georges for Michael as a birthday gift and we have been saving it separately from all our other wines for a special occasion.

This is that special occasion.

* * *

Michael has been moved now to a private ward in the Prince of Wales Hospital, our second home. I take in our bottle of wine and nice glasses. We pour the wine and it tastes awful, having become corked after being left for so long in the humidity of Hong Kong. We pull through the acute pain and poignancy of this 'bitter' moment.

Michael says, "It's the memory that counts."

He is right, although the knowledge that we might soon only have the memory is painful.

I also take a bottle of our favourite champagne, but even this no longer tastes good to Michael as he is attached to so many tubes and taking so much medication that he has lost his 'normal' sense of taste. Again, we feel the poignancy of this moment.

Each of these intense moments is a lesson in living and one that strikes our friends when we tell them. To quote our friend Jilly:

> We were actually talking about Michael last night; we had friends over for a drink on the roof and we had a bottle of champagne in the fridge. So we now use Michael as our reason or as our excuse: If there is a bottle of champagne in the fridge, we open it and finish it, because what are we saving it for?
>
> The story behind this was Sandra and Michael had a special bottle of wine that they had saved... and when Michael was in the hospital, they were having a nice picnic together and had Michael's favourite food, such as smoked salmon and all these nice things, but the wine was corked.
>
> It's such a strong metaphor for when we save things , but when we go to enjoy them, time's passed and it's already gone.

Ceci shows me a very moving film of a dying woman who makes a decision to hold her funeral whilst she is still alive so that she can be present to hear what she means to others and to feel surrounded and held by the love of her family in the final stages of her life. It is a large and special ceremony held at the university. This process is a positive and supportive one to all involved. Shortly after the funeral, the wife dies peacefully in her husband's arms.

I talk to Michael about some of Ceci's lovely experiences of communities coming together in ways that could be very loving for him, as our friends keep asking to see him.

He says, "I can't imagine anything worse. What do you mean? People are going to stand around me with balloons and I'll sit in a chair and watch them all having good fun and then they'll go away?"

For Michael, instead of seeing this as a positive experience, he is absolutely horrified. I feel so very sad. One of my struggles is that Michael has so many people whom he has inspired wanting to see him, to be with him, to have an opportunity to say goodbye and to thank him for the impact that he has had on their lives. Yet he does not want to see or be with anyone.

We talk through many different ideas. Our friend Terry has kindly suggested that perhaps a few friends just be with him and talk about everyday issues.

Michael says, "I don't want people to sit in the room and pretend like everything is ok, to chat socially. I don't want that. I don't want people not to know what to say."

Basically, Michael's objections end all forms of human communication methods that I know. Recognising just how strong his wishes are, I decide to stop searching.

Instead, I continue to keep friends away. There is one unplanned moment when I allow a good friend Joe, who has been by our side day-in and day-out, unfaltering in his support, to enter Michael's hospital room to help me with something. I let Michael know in advance. Joe steps briefly into the room to assist me.

Michael sees Joe and he draws all his energy together to open up and say, "Thank you for everything, Joe."

I know that these words come from the very depth of Michael's heart and soul, and how much it has taken out of him to speak them. He is saying goodbye and thank you as he experiences his own dying.

Joe is focused on supporting me and he does not really hear Michael. He completes the task and leaves the room, obviously concerned not to disturb Michael. There is absolutely no ill intent on Joe's part whatsoever. He was seeking to show his respect for Michael.

Michael turns to me after Joe leaves the room and says, "See what I mean?"

I do see and hear what he means. I am living Michael's dying, moment to moment, by his side. I am seeing life from a different perspective. There are very real instances when I feel like I am actually dying with him. In this poignant moment, I see the communication gulf separating where Michael is in living his dying from the world of friends and family that he so desperately doesn't want to leave and that he has fought so hard to stay with. I can't imagine the pain of seeing the people you love around you and knowing that you are leaving them forever. I now resolve to completely remove all forms of pressure from Michael and not to seek to influence him to change or to think differently. From now on, I am the gatekeeper holding the love and comments of friends and protecting Michael's space.

I talk with Terry and explain that I've exhausted every avenue in trying to arrange that endings with friends would be a positive experience for Michael, and that I have finally understood that this is not going to happen, that he is too far removed from our everyday world already. I ask Terry to please help me to help others understand that it will be important for them to find other ways to say goodbye. I can only ask for the understanding of friends.

Philippe helps me with this too when he says, "Michael is in a different place from us now. He is beyond us. He has moved on."

I take Michael his favourite foods, like Scottish smoked salmon, and bring in some DVDs that we enjoy watching. The last series we watch together is *Lost*. We have been awaiting the dramatic ending.

One night after the hospital I am so exhausted that I watch the ending as a special treat. Now when Michael asks if we can watch the ending together, I explain that I have seen it and am also happy to watch it again. Michael feels so very angry that I did not wait to share this ending with him. I had not meant to upset him but, suddenly realising how insensitive my action was, I am cross with myself that I did not fully think through the consequences of my behaviour. I am tired and indeed lost in learning how to navigate this totally new experience.

To help to ease the pain for Michael, I think very carefully about every word that I say and how I say it. This is difficult. I inadvertently mention looking forward to seeing the next series of *Lost* and immediately feel dreadful that such words have come out of my mouth. What am I doing, talking about looking ahead at a time like this—how insensitive can I be? In everyday life, such flow of conversation is normal yet not now, not when Michael knows that he no longer faces a future here on earth.

I feel some consolation when one of the hospice nurses comes in to visit us and her eyes fill with tears. She tells me that she has never, ever, in all her years of working, seen two people who are going through so much at this stage in someone's dying of cancer, show so much love, care and consideration to each other.

One of the questions that I ask Ceci—as I go to so much effort for us to look after Michael, to share enjoyable and special moments at this time—is, "How is it possible to experience fun and happiness, to feel such feelings when actually we mostly feel pain?"

Ceci talks with me of the 'bittersweet' experience. The feelings in sharing these moments together are not the same as having fun, yet what they do allow is some more sweetness amidst all the bitter feelings. This explanation makes sense to me. The mix of emotions that I typically feel—a heady cocktail of fear, pain, anger and guilt—is indeed a bitter experience. I can understand how introducing more sweetness can help to take the edge off this.

There are other ways that we introduce sweetness into these last times together as a family.

Ceci suggests, "You might want to create a family photo album together."

I discuss this idea with Diana. She immediately likes it, in part, because it is a practical and fun activity that will engage her in drawing and cutting things out. I take down a book that has been on my shelves for a long time, believing it to be empty. When I open it I find paintings in it, reflections on living and dying that Diana and I had started to work on several years earlier when we had begun to express our thoughts and feelings about her dad's illness through drawing. I had kept the book in a special place and had then forgotten about it. It is the perfect book in which we can now create an album of memories.

Diana suggests that we can get other people to contribute to the book. Picking up on her great suggestion, I e-mail friends to tell them about the book.

Diana says, "Mummy, I've got my own e-mail address so they can write to me."

So it is that the album becomes a positive focus for our family and community, taking its own shape and shared by each of us.

Ceci has introduced Diana and me to a lovely child psychologist called Alicia, who will help to support Diana through play therapy. Alicia comes to the hospital to be with Diana for a while. She enters the room with us both and holds Michael's hand. As she takes his hand, she looks up at me and says, "It's so cold."

I nod. Her response is a natural one and as she makes it, she realises what the implications of this are.

She looks at me gently with kind eyes and then says to Michael,

"Michael, please know that I am here to support Sandra and Diana and that I will look after them both."

Alicia's response reminds me how very close to Michael's dying we now are. I have grown so familiar with his body becoming colder and colder that I no longer notice or am startled by this in the way that she is.

I have brought a CD player into the room so that Michael and I can listen to music together. It has become more and more difficult for us both to listen to music and I believe that this is because music touches us so deeply that it becomes increasingly overwhelming to listen to, given the depth of the emotions that we are already connected with. Michael and I eventually can no longer bear to listen to music. Indeed it is also a long time before I do so again.

The last song that we listen to together is 'The Power of Love' by Jennifer Rush. Earlier, my friend Charles—who first introduced us to the only friends we knew when we arrived in Hong Kong— wrote an e-mail to me, saying: 'Remain open to the power of love, which is stronger than death.' His words resonate within me as Michael and I listen to the words and music of the song together for the last time. I play the song loud as I lie by Michael's side on his hospital bed and hold him as close as all the tubes will allow.

Saying Goodbye
September 2007

We're heading for something
Somewhere I've never been
Sometimes I am frightened
But I'm ready to learn about the power of love.

Jennifer Rush
'The Power of Love'

Ceci recommends a structured exercise using five sentences developed by Ira Byock, MD, in the USA that might help us to say goodbye. I explain this to Michael and ask if he is open to working with this framework. He is.

We take it in turns to follow each topic in the structure, to speak and to listen to each other. The first one is **"I love you."** In some ways, this is, of course, easy to say, as we love each other very much, yet in this context the words are deeply moving.

The second is **"Please forgive me."** When Ceci first presents this topic, I wonder why we need to spend so much time on forgiveness. Now I know. I had not realised just how many things were stored in my mind for which I wanted to ask Michael's forgiveness.

The third is **"I forgive you."**

Michael says, "There is nothing that you have said or done in our marriage for which I do not forgive you."

To hear him say, and to truly mean this, having heard all of the things that I have just spoken to him about, brings me closure. To this day, when thoughts pop into my mind of things that I wish I hadn't felt or done, I hear Michael's words and I absolutely know that he forgives me. I know this for sure.

The fourth is **"Thank you."** We each take a long time over this one. The final topic is to say "**Goodbye.**" We are not ready for this.

I am so deeply grateful for the closure that this structured framework of five sentences gives us at this time, and I also want to create an opportunity for Michael and Diana to say goodbye. Diana is not always at the hospital with us. One day, I make a special invitation for her to join us to say goodbye to Daddy, choosing to do so when he is still lucid. Diana and Michael are both quite shy and don't find it easy to talk about their feelings. As a result, they are in the room together, looking at each other, with each other, yet not really speaking or knowing what to do.

I seek to facilitate the conversation between them, drawing on years of professional training. "Maybe there are things that you and Daddy would like to say to each other?"

Then Diana takes the lead. She sits down beside Michael, reaches to take his hand in hers, looks him straight in the eye and says, "I love you Daddy."

With my own eyes full to the brim with tears, drawing from Ceci's teaching, I say to Michael, "Maybe you would like to tell Diana some of the things that you'd like her to take into life."

Michael continues to look directly at Diana with her hand in his. He says, "I love you Diana." He thinks some more and then says, "The most important thing that I want you to take into life is to teach yourself. Never believe that anyone else has the answers. Listen to yourself, learn, be open to learning, but be your own teacher, respect yourself and be your own teacher. Don't look to others to give you the answers."

Diana hangs on to his every word. I hang on to his every word. She looks at him and nods.

Michael says, "Diana, are you listening?"

She nods intently. Then Diana turns to me and in a curious voice—nothing more, just curious—says, "Mummy, why have we never done this before?" I am filled with wonder and amazement at the poignant simplicity of her comment.

Diana also, completely unprompted, selects a really soft pale-blue teddy bear, brings it into the ward and lays it beside her daddy for him to cuddle.

Michael says, "Thank you, Diana."

Ceci says, "The one thing that people often miss the most after someone dies is the sound of their voice. I suggest that you record your conversations now so that you will always have these when your memory fades."

I am not good with technology. This is Michael's skill in our family. This suggestion is one step too far for me. There is just so much for me to organise and do that the very thought of working out where to find recording equipment and then how to use it, just feels like simply too much. I give up on this idea, and I regret this now. Ceci is right.

Michael's mother, his brother William and his Aunt Jeanette are with us now, having flown across from Glasgow. They each in their turn spend private time with Michael. When I tell Michael's mother, a few days earlier, that Michael is asking for his brother, she knows that it is time for her to come out to Hong Kong. Don't ask me how. A mother just knows. Michael's family arrives just in time to have a couple of days with him to say goodbye when he is lucid, after which he starts to depart from us. One of Michael's closest friends from childhood, Stewart, also flies out to be with him at this time. In Stewart's own words: "Being able to tell him I love him and him back at me in those hours prior to his passing was incredibly important to me and I thank you for allowing me to speak with him, albeit that he was so incredibly exhausted."

As with all families at a time like this one, we are all under a great deal of stress and I am eternally grateful that friends are by our side and that they help with the care of Michael's family.

Joe arranges with a colleague to borrow a car and driver to bring Michael's family to the hospital each day. This practical support holds a value way beyond words as the hospital is a long way from our home.

Our Scottish neighbour, Ian, and his wife Aileen, cook up a thick soup to feed us all when we get home. How much more support can a friend give than good, warm, home-cooked food served with a Glaswegian accent in Tong Fuk Village! Talk about home away from home!

Michael's mother is in an understandable state of complete distress and my friends recognise that it will put too much pressure on me to support her. So does Michael's Aunt Jeanette who is such a kind and incredibly practical woman. She takes charge of supporting Michael's mother and brother.

For the most part, we manage fairly effectively as a distraught family, apart from at one potentially explosive moment, which I write about now by way of showing how easy it is for family members to fall out when all are together yet each is in his own grief process— together yet alone.

There are a few hours in the hospital when we leave Michael and his mother alone. She is a devout Catholic but Michael made a very clear and conscious decision to leave the Catholic Church in his youth. All Michael's friends and family know his views on Catholicism and how important these are to him.

When we return to the hospital, the nurses on the ward take me to one side.

"Michael's mother has requested that he see a priest yet Michael has never asked to see a priest. Is this something that he wants?"

Thank goodness that the nurses handle this situation with such professionalism and diplomacy, protecting Michael's rights in this way. I speak with Michael, explaining that his mother would like him to see a priest and asking if this is what he wants. His words are very clear: "No. I don't want to see a priest."

I explain this sensitive situation to Jeanette and William who both rise immediately to the occasion with wonderful strength, totally understanding and respecting Michael's rights. They empathise. They support Michael's mother, leaving me free to support Michael.

Later, one of the nurses asks if it would be okay to invite her friend to cut Michael's hair. I am grateful for this, as I have been asking if there is a hospital hairdresser, to no avail. Next morning, I arrive to find Michael with a very smart new haircut. He tells me that the person who cut his hair asked if it would be okay to say a prayer with him and that he had accepted this request.

From now on, we move into the final stages of Michael's life. I have never been alongside someone dying, let alone someone whom I love so much. I am eternally grateful that those for whom this is a more familiar experience are beside me to teach me.

There are some particularly shocking moments when Michael starts to panic as his lungs are filling up with cancer and he can't breathe. In these moments I start to panic, too.

Ceci says, "Learning to deal with breathlessness is an important and natural part of dying. Reassure Michael. Remind him to please be calm and encourage him to take deep breaths. Explain how feeling frightened will make things worse, perhaps fan him and open the windows. Remind him that he has all the air that he needs."

This kind of simple, factual information is exactly what I need to hear. Feelings of fear give way to straightforward tasks and actions, with which I am engaged.

The other people who teach me now are Michael's doctors. There are now two main doctors in charge: the palliative care oncologist and Michael's orthopaedic surgeon who is continuing to follow up on the pelvic surgery.

The oncologist takes me to one side and says, "It is clear that Michael trusts you. I would like to suggest that I teach you how to support Michael and that you be the person at his side. He will then feel most comfortable and I can be here for you."

Her intervention is deeply sensitive, caring, the best possible intervention. She explains to me about the morphine that they are giving Michael for his pain and tells me, "Trust your own judgment as you are with him. You will know when he needs more pain relief."

As Michael drifts further and further out of consciousness, he is less and less able to speak. At times when he can, he is fairly lucid. On one such occasion, he tells me that he feels frightened and that he doesn't want to leave us.

I say, "Michael, I don't want you to leave us either, yet when the time is right, I am also ready to let you go." He tosses and turns.

I say to him, "I know that you don't want to leave us and that the thought of leaving us is frightening. For a moment, instead of looking at what you are leaving behind, I'd like to suggest that you look ahead to your next step. What do you see? Where is your path taking you next? What image do you hold of this next step? Is this a frightening image?"

Michael's eyes fill with tears, as do mine, as he replies simply, "I know that I am going home."

From this point onwards, it is as if Michael starts to gradually let go. I sit by his side. I mop his brow with damp cloths. I support his breathing. And the oncologist is right: there is one significant moment when Michael is tossing and turning more than I have seen him do before. He cannot speak, yet he communicates—and I hear. I call the doctor.

"Help! I think that Michael is in too much pain."

She arrives quickly to assess the situation, tells me that my judgment is correct and administers more morphine.

Michael's orthopaedic surgeon is also coaching me. He encourages me, whilst he talks about what I am likely to see over the coming hours. He provides me with factual information as if I were a nursing or medical student. I feel empowered. I feel respected and I learn fast. I don't want to be anywhere other than right here right now, and it means a great deal to me that the professionals around me are teaching me how to be here in the best possible way for Michael. This kind of simplified factual information is exactly what I need so that I do not feel frightened and overwhelmed. Dying is a process that the doctors and nurses have seen many times before and I have not.

I make arrangements to sleep on the sofa in Michael's room, although sleep proves to be pretty much elusive. I sense every move that Michael makes. I am afraid to close my eyes in case he is not there when I awaken. No one expects him to live through the night. Michael is not able to communicate through words and it becomes increasingly difficult for him to take in water.

In the morning, I sit alongside his bed. The orthopaedic surgeon enters the room. I am aware of his presence, although I do not turn to him to speak. I am in an intense emotional state, in part through sheer exhaustion and, in part, through what I can only refer to as some kind of attunement with Michael's dying process. It is as if I am in a daze.

Michael has been tossing and turning all night. His breakfast tray arrives, although this is pretty useless given that he is not able to eat. I am fussing around, leaning over Michael and organising what to do with the tray when he pushes the top half of his body up on the bed and kisses me on the cheek. He then immediately collapses down into what looks like a state of oblivion.

I wonder for a split second if I have just imagined what happened. As I feel Michael's kiss, in the same way that I intuitively knew when he was in too much pain, I intuitively know that he is saying goodbye. My eyes fill with tears.

The orthopaedic surgeon speaks with me later: "I have never, in all my years of medicine, seen a man in this stage of dying do what Michael just did."

I sit by Michael's bedside, as I have done so many times, with my laptop on my knee, managing the many different tasks that I need to coordinate. Shortly after lunch, I am e-mailing family and friends when I look up, sensing that something has changed. A nurse walks into the room at that same moment. She checks Michael's pulse.

There is no pulse. The nurse leaves and I climb into bed with Michael. His body still holds some warmth and in that moment, it seems to me that Michael's spirit is still with me. I whisper, "Goodbye, Michael. I love you very much."

Michael has died. Diana's soft blue teddy bear is still at his side.

Family Photographs

Sharm el Sheikh, Egypt 1991
Sandra, single before meeting
Michael, aged 27

London, UK 1992
Sandra, aged 28 and Michael,
aged 31; after meeting in
1992

Bolton, UK, 6th February 1993
Sandra and Michael's wedding day

Dunstable, UK 1994
Sandra and Michael's
1st wedding anniversary

UK, 1999
Sandra and Michael together
with their daugther,
Diana Marie Keys
(b. 12th Janurary 1999)

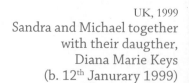

Iceland, 1999
Michael and Diana at a
friend's wedding in Iceland
shortly before moving to
Hong Kong

Hong Kong, December, 1999
Michael in hospital for
heart surgery, with Diana
at his side

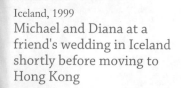

Hong Kong, 12th January 2000
Celebrating Diana's
1st birthday together
in hospital

Hong Kong, 2000
Diana with her daddy at his office

Scotland, UK, November 2000
Michael with his mum, dad and Diana

Bolton, UK, November 2000
Sandra's mum and dad with Diana

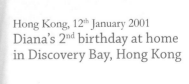

Hong Kong, 12th January 2001
Diana's 2nd birthday at home in Discovery Bay, Hong Kong

Hong Kong, June 2001
Monday Baby Group Children

Hong Kong, January 2001
Charles, Jeremy, Debra,
Colin, Michael and Sandra at
the China Club

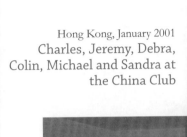

Hong Kong, 22nd March 2001
Michael's 40th birthday at
home in Discovery Bay

London, November 2001
Karen and Diana in the
local Indian restaurant on
Clapham High Street

Hong Kong, August 2002
Michael back in hospital for
reconstructive stomach surgery,
with Sandra at his side

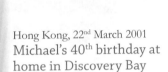

Hong Kong, August 2002
Michael in hospital with
Diana at his side

Hong Kong, September 2002
Debra and Colin leaving
Hong Kong; Michael just out
of hospital

Hong Kong, Christmas 2002
Diana and Paige in
Tung Chung

Hong Kong , December 2003
Sandra and Michael

Hong Kong, circa 2003
Michael and Harold

Hong Kong, circa 2003
Michael with colleagues and their families from Harold Crowter Associates at the Happy Valley races

Discovery Bay, Hong Kong, 2003
Mothers and children in the Monday Baby Group; one member, Alison, and her family is absent

South Lantau, Hong Kong, 2007
Sandra, Michael and Diana, after the amputation of Michael's leg and the last family photo taken before his death

Michael Brennan Keys
22nd March 1961 — 6th September 2007

Hong Kong, 2007
Sandra and Diana arriving
back to Hong Kong just after
Michael's funeral in Scotland

Hong Kong, October 2007
Memorial Beach Ceremony
for Michael in Tong Fuk

Hong Kong, October 2007
Diana and her friends dancing
in Michael's Memorial Beach
Ceremony

Hong Kong, Summer 2008
Sandra's cousin Trevor, his
wife Lynne and two boys
Thomas and Michael in
Hong Kong with her and
Diana

Hong Kong, 6th September 2008
Sandra with Justina in
Hong Kong on the first
anniversary after Michael
and TP's deaths

Hong Kong, 6th September 2008
Diana and Susanne
ice skating together in
Hong Kong on the first
Anniversary of Michael's
death

Mui Wo, Hong Kong,
6th September 2008
Sandra and Diana buying
a special Chinese cabinet
with Paddy and Barbara in
memory of Michael on the
first anniversary of his death

Scotland, Christmas 2009
Sandra with her sister Alison

Scotland, Christmas 2009
Diana with her cousins Ben
and Rory

Scotland, December 2009
Sandra and Diana visiting
Michael's grave for the first
time since his funeral

Tong Fuk, Hong Kong, February 2010
Dwight, Jenny and Diana
together at home on Jenny's
birthday

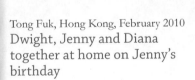

London, January 2010
Sandra with Valerie celebrating
their birthdays together

Manila, February 2010
Sandra aged 46 and Diana aged 11,
celebrating Chinese New Year
(the Year of Tiger)

Repatriating Michael's Body Home to Scotland
September 2007 cont.

Where me and my true love will never meet again,
On the bonnie, bonnie banks of Loch Lomond.

Runrig
'Loch Lomond'

I learn a profound lesson in the moment of Michael's dying. Death in itself is a moment; it is the moment when someone stops breathing. This fact, in itself, simply 'is'.

I have walked every step of the way with Michael until his dying breath and when this moment is past, the next moment emerges, just like any other moment in time.

We fear death; we hide it in taboo corners of our existence and for what, for why? In the hands of teachers, I have learned that dying and death is a process: it is a process that we can learn about, that we can support others and ourselves with and that, in and of itself, it simply is a fact—nothing more and nothing less. I have just faced the 'imaginary monster hidden in the corner' and have emerged stronger and wiser.

My friend Rachel calls me shortly after Michael dies and later reports her experience of this call:

> I remember calling you, the first time that I spoke to you after Michael died, so we'd been in text contact but we hadn't actually spoken and I was really nervous because I was thinking, "What am I going to say?" I know I want to be there and I want to be supportive and I know that you may want to talk, you may not want to talk. If you do want to talk, how do I facilitate that without being patronising, without being "Oh, there, there,

there..." whatever... so... okay... Well, we're going to do this, come on, we're going to make the call.

You answered the phone and I just said something like "How is it?" or "How are you?" and you just started talking me very naturally through the learning that you had through Michael's death, through the thanking and the forgiving, and I was blown away.

I came out of that call feeling uplifted. I felt that something that I had been really scared of had turned into, for me, a very life-affirming experience. And that was something that I had been dreading so much and yet you made it into something that I came away with the biggest learning of my life. It was very powerful.

Whilst on the one hand I do feel empowered, on the other I am totally and utterly exhausted and all that I want to do is to collapse and sleep for a million years. Yet, this is not a time for me to collapse. Michael's wish is to be buried near his parents' home in Bridge of Weir in Scotland. I want to honour his wish so it is now my responsibility to return his body to Scotland—yet another 'first' for me!

Two striking things happen almost immediately after Michael dies. The first is that his mother and Aunt Jeanette decide to catch the earliest flight out of Hong Kong that they can and William is asked to go, despite the fact that he has made plans to take Diana to Disneyland for the weekend. These are cancelled.

The second is that, immediately after they leave, Joe calls to inform me that he has cancelled the car that had been kindly loaned to our family for a week, even though we have not yet reached the end of that week. He does this because the company lent us the car whilst Michael's mother was here and he knows that she is returning to Scotland.

I steadily remind myself that I am not completely and utterly alone. Paddy encourages me to phone Joe to ask if I can have the support of the car for one more day as there is so much that I need to arrange. Joe very kindly helps me out with this.

The day after Michael dies, I return to the hospital alone to visit the mortuary and to sort out the paperwork. This is a kind of final journey that I want to make alone. It is an important ritual of saying farewell when I sign the paperwork with the man at the desk.

Afterwards, I sit alone on the plastic chairs in the corridor by the

Accident and Emergency ward, and I reflect. I have spent so much of my life pacing these corridors. I am now leaving the hospital too: another ending. As I sit in quiet contemplation, the orthopaedic surgeon walks by reception, sees me and sits down. He tells me he has recently given a presentation on the treatment of leiomyosarcoma and that Michael's name was on the list—amongst those of doctors—of the people who have contributed to this field. He tells me how a part of Michael's legacy will be to inform the treatment of leiomyosarcoma in years to come. I feel very proud. I say goodbye.

Whilst returning my husband's body to the UK is a 'first' for me, managing repatriation in this way is not a 'first' for Paddy who, thankfully, takes over in the gentlest and most supportive of ways. Paddy has already done the research. He is ready. He knows who to contact and he sets all the practical motions in place. I feel totally and utterly held by his strength. I don't have to take a lead; I have to follow instructions, which is a considerable relief.

Colin sends us his air miles, which combined with some of my own, enables us to upgrade to Business Class. We have never travelled Business Class before. I feel so grateful and, in a strange way, this makes the trip a special one, however painful it is to be again 'walking in the shadow of death'.

The next practical task on my agenda is to visit the funeral parlour here in Hong Kong.

Ceci says, "Find ways to practically engage and involve Diana in the process. Perhaps she can film the funeral so that she can be present yet also have a practical role to play?"

How different this suggestion is from when I was a child!

* * *

My first experience of death is when I am around three years old or so. I can't remember my exact age, yet I do vividly remember that day. I am with my mum and don't remember my sister being with me so I might have been even younger.

As soon as we arrive at Grandma's house, I run up the stairs to her bedroom. I shake her arm to awaken her to play. She does not stir. I run downstairs to tell Mum that Granny will not wake up. My mum runs upstairs and the next thing that I know, not through words that are spoken to me, but through all my senses, is that something is terribly wrong. I hear my mum's voice on the phone. I feel frightened. My Aunty Joyce, who lives just up the road, arrives and I am ushered into different rooms.

Later I learn that Granny has died and this is the last time that I am being engaged in this process in any way. My first experience of death, then, is of something very frightening, so frightening, in fact, that adults don't even talk about it as they themselves are afraid.

* * *

I speak with Philippe, who is a documentary filmmaker, about Ceci's idea for Diana to film the funeral. He thinks this is a great suggestion and helps to teach Diana how to use our video camera. He notes that she has a natural eye for filming.

* * *

It is interesting to me that, as I write this section of my book, I feel a similar kind of weary exhaustion wash over me as I experienced at this time. I don't want to write the words in the same way that I don't want to take the steps. Normally a practical person, I find that doing tasks comes easily to me. Now each one seems completely overwhelming. I move slowly, one step at a time, as if in a waking dream.

* * *

Ceci says, "Bereaved people are like disabled people, only no one can see your disability. Bereaved people are more prone to accidents. You need to take extra special care of yourself. It is important not to drive."

I am so grateful when our friend Marie asks if she can accompany Diana and me to the funeral parlour. Diana films the trip. One of the fascinating and wonderful things about Hong Kong is that you have streets together where all the shops sell the same things. So, if you want to buy bathroom sinks and taps then you know to go to a particular area of Wan Chai. What I didn't know is that it is exactly the same for funeral parlours and flowers, which are all together in one area of the city.

The streets here are busy and have the most wonderful array of wreaths. The funeral parlour is large and there is a Buddhist ceremony taking place as we walk through the building. Incense fills the air. There are large, purpose-built anterooms with framed pictures of loved ones. Diana films as we walk and talk. It is like a strange, yet also especially important, family outing. The funeral director shows us a wooden box that is ready to be shipped. I show this to Diana, explaining how Daddy's body will go in a box like this one.

As we learn ourselves about a process that neither Marie nor I have engaged in before, we also seek to teach Diana, to exchange some of the fear for simple facts. Marie encourages Diana to have her photo taken as a distraction from the constant zoom on our faces! Diana, however, feels more comfortable behind the camera. The idea of her filming in this way is inspired.

I talk with Diana in the lift about all the photos and e-mails coming through from family and friends for her to put in our memory book.

As we open the door of the lift, Marie says, "Listen, bagpipes!"

I am amazed even now by the poignancy of this moment. Here, in one of the busiest areas of Hong Kong, bagpipe music is being played on one of the floors. The clatter, the noise, the chaos, the bustle, the Chinese accents and the red taxis all provide comfort to me. All are now familiar and welcoming.

I hear myself now talking from the taxi home with my colleague Vivian about action that we need to take over a business project that she has suddenly relieved me of responsibility for, and I find it hard to imagine how it is possible to stay grounded as these days pass. I let more and more of my work go and remain deeply grateful that Neil, Vivian and Pennie simply, and without question, step in to remove this considerable weight from my shoulders. As a director of a small business, it would be easy to feel alone, so I particularly value the teamwork from colleagues who stand by me through personal choice and friendship, and not because of any stipulated employer requirement.

Whilst I am making the necessary arrangements to fly Michael's body to the UK, his Aunt Jeanette is with Michael's mum and brother, organising the funeral arrangements in Scotland with great care and efficiency. Michael's mother has already reserved a grave for Michael. He will be buried with his dad. Jeanette and I are in constant contact.

Marie gives Diana and me a gift of an Ian Rankin novel, *Exit Music*, at this time. She knows how Michael had always loved to read his books. She writes: "It seems somehow apt Rebus will probably not appear in any more of Rankin's novels. I know how much Michael enjoyed to read them."

Before leaving I send out the invitations to Michael's funeral. For a long time, I have also been imagining a ceremony that I would like to hold here on the beach in Tong Fuk Village for all those who have been beside us as our 'family' here in Hong Kong. I really want this for our friends and for me, and so I set a date in October 2007, shortly after we are due to return from Scotland.

To our friends, this seems a very long time away, whereas I have no idea exactly how I shall organise this within such a short timescale. I only know how much I want this ceremony. The funeral is a ritual that is expected of me, that I must somehow go through. My limited experience of funerals is that they are painful and unbearable events. My creative thoughts for Michael's beach ceremony are very different: they represent my innermost longing, the path of my own healing and the way that I want to say goodbye—and although only images in my mind, they are strong images.

It is whilst planning the funeral, repatriation and flight arrangements, as well as writing and speaking to friends and family that I face one more acutely painful moment.

My dad calls me, "Sandra, I don't think that I'm going to make it to Michael's funeral. It's such a long way up to Scotland. I hope that you understand."

My dad has been through so much in caring for my mum; he is elderly and tired. In the normal run of events I probably would understand, yet not in this moment. In this moment I don't understand at all. At other times, I might push my own feelings to one side and show empathy and understanding for my dad—but not now. I burst into tears and feel angry.

My dad is very upset. He doesn't want me to react in this way. Again, I see how family relationships can easily be at breaking point at highly emotional times such as these. Thankfully, my sister steps in and speaks with my cousin Gillian who offers to give my dad a lift up to Scotland.

And so it is that Diana and I finally head to the airport together. I feel very relieved that Michael, or rather Michael's body—it is still difficult to distinguish between the two at this stage—is travelling on a different flight, due to arrive in Scotland before us.

The words of the song 'Loch Lomond' float through my mind. Michael is the first man to show me the 'steep sides of Ben Lomond'. Past memories of Scotland fill my mind as we put our feet up in Business Class. I am returning to Scotland's shores, where I shall never again meet Michael. This very thought itself is excruciating.

Michael's Funeral in Renfrew
September 2007 cont.

An honest man here lies at rest
As e'er God with his image blest;
The friend of man, the friend of truth,
The friend of age, and guide of youth:
Few hearts like his, with virtue warm'd,
Few heads with knowledge so inform'd:
If there's another world, he lives in bliss;
If there is none, he made the best of this.

Robert Burns
'Epitaph on my own Friend'

My sister buys me a beautiful book of Scottish laments. The verse above, which our friend Bryce later reads at Michael's beach ceremony in Tong Fuk, is in it.

Diana and I relax on the flight, a very unfamiliar experience for me at this stage. We are looked after with real care and attention in Business Class and I have asked Jenny to travel with us for support. This is also a very emotional time for Jenny as well: she has been a part of our family for many years now. The flight is long. The wait at Heathrow and the connecting flight from London to Edinburgh feel unbearable. We are to stay with my sister Ali who lives in a little Scottish seaside town called Dunbar. I know that we will all feel relaxed with my sister and her husband John, and that Diana will enjoy the company of her two young cousins, Ben and Rory. John has kindly offered to drive us all to Glasgow together for the funeral.

Ali meets us at the airport and we drive to her home. From the moment we arrive at Ali's home, I feel relief. I feel the warmth of the central heating. I focus on the 'here and now'. I have all the paperwork.

I have English currency. I have my Blackberry and mobile phone to keep me connected. I have the book of Scottish laments that my sister has given to me. I lay all these items out in my bedroom and unpack. I love hearing the noise of Diana playing with her cousins. I begin to settle and to feel new ground beneath my feet.

We go to the supermarket so I can buy all the food that I miss. I feel comforted by the smells and sounds of Jenny cooking familiar food in Ali's kitchen. I open cards that have been sent to us and display them above Ali's fireplace. I love that she and John allow me to feel at home in this way. We put out flowers that have arrived. A colleague from Hong Kong sent me a CD that I have brought with me to Scotland and my sister and I stretch out on her sofas to listen to it. It is called *Hope* by Gretchen Harris.

There are lots of e-mails, calls and messages from friends and family travelling to the funeral yet I experience these as going on around me in a different orbit. I want everyone to take responsibility for himself now. I can feel myself starting to flag, wanting to put down the heavy weight of responsibility that I have shouldered for so long, wanting to throw it away. I continue to manage tasks and actions while longing not to have to. I feel ungrateful feeling this way then, and still do now, writing about those feelings. I remind myself that my friends are coming to Scotland because they care for and love Michael, Diana and me. I keep my act together whilst yearning to stay curled up on the sofa with the music, my sister, the noise of the children playing and the warmth of the central heating—and to shut the rest of my experience and the world out.

The day of Michael's funeral dawns...

And I would rather be anywhere else but here today...

Elvis Costello and The Attractions
'Oliver's Army'

Although I have been slowing down and sleeping, albeit whilst battling with jet lag, I feel the inner pressure and tension rise as the day of Michael's funeral arrives and I am very grateful that Jeanette, and now my sister, help to shoulder the practical issues in Scotland.

I am concerned that I need to arrive in Glasgow early, as there are many matters to attend to before the funeral. I start to worry about the traffic. My sister has taken care of arranging the transport to ease my worries about having to drive or being late.

The trip from Edinburgh to Glasgow is short and one that I have made many times. Looking out of the window now, I see many familiar landmarks through new eyes, as I have never before travelled to Michael's home without him. His absence is palpable and painful.

We arrive at Michael's mum's house in Bridge of Weir. Diana knows her granny's house well, and she is both with her family and Jenny, and also continuing to film. Her role as filmmaker enables her to be a part of the day whilst also putting space between herself and others in being behind the camera. I imagine that she is better able to handle her feelings in this way. I am deeply grateful to her for this now as the films bring back memories of aspects of that day which would otherwise be submerged in the pain.

Michael's mum and Aunt Jeanette are busy preparing sandwiches and cakes, and serving endless cups of tea. Michael's family has arrived from Ireland. I don't know them well but I do have fond memories of our trip to Ireland and know how much time spent with his family there meant to Michael. They talk about how good it was to see Michael looking so well at his dad's funeral. We all look at family photos on the wall and in albums. Diana films these as a record. I feel a bit as if I am participating in a surreal movie that I don't want to be a part of. I see now how my experience of the outer world then was a projection of inner pain that was too hard to bear in full.

It is difficult for me to be with Michael's mother who is in so much pain and often breaking into tears. Seeing her in this way reminds me of my own pain. It is still hard for me to watch Diana's films, now nearly two years after this time, yet I also experience some integration and sense of healing in doing so. Many of the photos are of loved ones no longer present.

I leave early for the funeral parlour. I have practical arrangements to make such as paying the bills, but, much more importantly, I want time alone with Michael's body.

The last time that I saw Michael's body was when he was transferred to the morgue in the Prince of Wales Hospital. I want to do this. I want to make sure that he has arrived.

The men in the funeral parlour prepare me for what to expect. I have seen dead bodies prepared and dressed only on TV. This is different. This is very real. Michael is dressed in the clothes that we packed for him in Hong Kong, including a Winnie the Pooh tie that Diana bought for him. His body is painted and it is clear to me that this is Michael's body, that I have done my job, that I have brought him home and that Michael is no longer with me. I tell him how much I love him, I welcome him home to Scotland and I say goodbye.

On my way out of this small room, I walk into Stewart, one of Michael's oldest and closest friends. I know why we are all here and I know who is coming, yet it is still strange to see him again now in Scotland after being with him earlier in the hospital in Hong Kong. Stewart says that he would like to see Michael. Afterwards Stewart says to me words to the effect of "It's what I have always believed: Mikey is no longer with us. His soul has left his body and it is only the physical remains that are here with us now."

My dad is the next person I meet. I feel relieved to have physical contact with him. Karen also arrives. Diana is hungry and we find a local Wimpy bar. Karen and I used to eat and drink in a Wimpy bar in Bolton when we were teenagers and had our first taste of freedom without parents while shopping in town on a Saturday afternoon. Fond memories of our childhood return to us as we tuck into our plate of chips.

I face a sea of familiar faces—family, old friends, new friends, people from different parts of the world who are all converging together for the first time in a car park outside a funeral parlour. Again, the experience is surreal and also supportive all at once: it is good to see everyone, including my brother (my birth mother Pauline's son) and his wife, whom I have never met before. He has been recently reunited with Pauline and comes along to support her. It is good, if strange, to meet him in this way.

Michael's funeral service is moving. The minister has taken care to learn about Michael's life and explains to people that Diana will be filming. Looking at the film later I see the dark rims beneath my eyes and my heavy lids. The simple, white floral displays from family bring beauty, life and comfort before us. It is a simple, practical chapel with tartan curtains and an organist. Diana captures the essence of this time with perfection.

Michael's casket is now closed. I know that his body is in there. We sing 'All Things Bright and Beautiful', a hymn I have chosen that holds special childhood memories for me. The traditional rituals lend support. The minister reminds us that today is the anniversary of our engagement in 1992. He reads a verse, 'Death Is Nothing At All', written by Canon Henry Scott-Holland:

> I have only slipped away into the next room
> I am I and you are you
> Whatever we were to each other
> That we are still.

As Michael's casket is removed from the funeral parlour, the strains of 'You'll Never Walk Alone' are played from the CD that I have brought with me from Hong Kong. It is now that the tears well in my eyes and stream down my face as I close my eyes and as my sister holds and hugs me. Until this moment, Diana and I have been sitting alone at the front of the chapel. I am so relieved to have her by my side as we walk first out of the chapel and as all the family and friends then come to greet us to pay their respects. Whilst the ritual is important, it is also formal and places a significant emotional burden on me. Thank goodness Jenny is here with us and will remain with us after everyone else leaves. Thank goodness that my closest friends are with me.

Amidst the heavy emotional load of the funeral, there are a couple of moments of humour. These are initially met with some feelings of embarrassment though, in truth, they afford some light relief. The one I shall never forget is as we make our way from the funeral parlour to the cemetery. At all the funerals that I have attended before, other cars have followed behind a cortege of the main funeral cars and the coffin. This is not the case here: family and friends are sharing cars and Michael's coffin is taken before they are organised. The result is that no one, aside from a handful of people who live locally, knows where we are going.

What follows are bizarre moments when I see family and friends from all around the world stopping at roundabouts and asking for directions to Houston Cemetery. I have only recently returned to Houston Cemetery and now have a better sense of where it is! Thankfully I am not driving so am able to watch this aspect of the proceedings more as an amused bystander.

The sunshine amidst the clouds holds out for most of the time at the cemetery. Although there are aspects of the funeral rituals which I find frightening, such as the formal mourning dress and some of the words and actions of the minister, nonetheless I welcome the opportunity to be by Michael's side for this final time as his body is lowered into the ground, as I throw soil over his coffin and as I say goodbye.

In this moment, Diana, who is cold and hungry, is eating a bag of chips from the Wimpy bar. How sad it seems to me that children have been excluded from these important events in the past, so much so that they become shrouded in mystery rather than being a communal and simple fact of life. This moment of Diana eating chips and standing with me and my friends chatting a little as we watch the formal proceedings, whilst she says goodbye to her dad, is one that deeply touches me and will stay in the memory of others as well.

The rain holds off until Michael's coffin and body are finally placed at rest. After the burial comes the 'funeral breakfast' as it is known in Scotland. This means that we all retire to a local pub in Renfrew that serves sausage rolls, sandwiches, warm cups of tea and also alcohol. I relax into this welcome, warm and comforting environment. I know that Diana relaxes too as we have no film of this part of the day. Friends whom I haven't seen for some time have travelled to be with us such as Lizzie, Jane and Mike, and Catriona and Deef. Valerie has brought her third son, baby Sam, with her. Diana loves to play with and care for Sam. It is truly an amazing experience to be surrounded by friends and family from all different stages in my and Michael's lives as we all share stories.

I am reminded as I write of my German friend Petra's words at a later date when we share our experiences of death and dying:

> There was my grandfather's funeral; I was six but I was not allowed to go—I'm still upset today ... All kids had to stay home. My granddad had had a heart attack ... so I wanted to be there ...

> All the relatives [were] there and I knew afterwards that they
> had [had] fun because [it is fun] whenever my Mum's side [gets
> together]. It is a huge family and some of these uncles and great
> uncles ... are quite some characters and they would start fighting
> within five minutes ... it was fun, honestly, it was. And we would
> laugh about it later on, make jokes ...
>
> "What did she say?"
>
> "What did he say?"
>
> You couldn't mention football [or] politics and they would be
> up the walls and it would happen at a funeral.

This part of the day really does feel like a party to me. I feel relief
that the formalities are over and that I am surrounded by people I
love. Throughout the whole event, however, I keep expecting Michael
to walk through the door and am shocked that he is not with us. I
keep thinking how much he would love to be here now.

I understand in this moment the real value of the family
gatherings, of the 'hatches, matches and dispatches', of the 21st, 40th
and 50th birthday parties. These matter because they can never be
recreated. The homemade video from our wedding is so special to me
now as there are people present who will never be present again.

Valerie (with Sam) and Karen have decided to stay on in Dunbar in
a lovely little hotel right on the coast near Ali's home. I feel so grateful
to them for staying on with me. Incredibly, what happens next is one
of the happiest and most special moments of my life. I am with three
women whom I love most and with some of our children: Diana, Ben,
Rory and Sam. We all hang out together. We take walks in the cold
wind along the Scottish shoreline. We eat lovely food watching the
night sky from the cliff-edge restaurant or curl up in the local bar
with pub lunches. Life is simple, relaxed and happy. It is a long time
since we have had the luxury of time together like this: truthfully we
have never had time exactly like this before. Even now, as I write, I
feel the same warmth inside, together with a sense of longing to have
this precious time again.

I also experience moments of acute pain and fear. One night
I awaken with a deep sense of fear that I don't know how I shall
send in my Hong Kong business tax returns in time. Thankfully,
nighttime in the UK is daytime in Hong Kong. I call Kate, who is very
knowledgeable on financial matters. She calms me down, explaining

rationally that I have some flexibility on timelines and don't need to panic. I feel relieved and go back to sleep.

For the most part, however, I allow myself to relax, as if leaning on a soft cushion that I haven't felt in a very long time. I am warm and cared for in my sister's home, with Ali and Jenny both pottering in the kitchen amidst the playful, sometimes loud, noises of the children. I love it. My deep, growing desire is never to leave.

Michael's Beach Ceremony in Hong Kong
October 2007

Decisions are only the beginning of something.
When someone makes a decision he is, in fact,
plunging into a powerful current
that carries him to a place
he had never even dreamed of
when he made that initial decision.

Paulo Coelho
The Alchemist

I dread our return to Hong Kong. I am no longer returning home; I am returning to the place where Michael and I established a home together. My home has always been a place of sanctuary; now it is an empty shell of memories and of jobs, tasks, responsibilities and fears that I have absolutely no desire to face. I dream of buying a home around the corner from my sister's house. But running away, although incredibly seductive as a fantasy, is simply not possible.

Thank goodness Colin and Paddy have helped arrange Business Class flights as the momentary comfort of full-length beds, champagne and movies during this nightmare of a transition helps me to focus my mind, reminding me to live in the 'here and now' reality—which is actually very luxurious—in order to prevent myself from feeling completely overwhelmed.

As we touch down, I feel the pleasure of walking out into the gentle autumn warmth and remember that this is my favourite season in Hong Kong. The city's skyline has also become one of my favourite sights and I feel more relaxed when I see it again. I have been living here nearly eight years by this time. Gently, I allow myself to breathe in and out, minute to minute, focusing simply and gradually only on whatever faces me in the present. In so doing, I feel my feet firmly on the ground and I start to navigate this particularly difficult transition.

I have the project of Michael's Beach Ceremony on which to focus my attention. Why have I given myself this additional pressure? Am I completely mad? This ceremony holds a deep and profound importance for me, and I want to provide an opportunity for our community to mourn—especially as so many people who cared so much for Michael were unable to say goodbye to him in person. Now is the moment for me to translate vision into action. Now I shall experience the absolute, total and mind-blowing support of our community around me.

The first people who approach me to help are my close women friends from Tong Fuk—Malou, Stella, Grace and Cristina. Malou explains that they all want to help to organise Michael's ceremony and they ask me what they can do. She suggests that she be the lead link person to me and that they take care of the food, flowers and decorations.

I cannot think of anything more wonderful or any team better skilled for this particular role. Malou, Stella and Grace are all Filipino women who bring an indescribable Asian grace and beauty to the presentation of food and flowers, unlike anything that I have seen in my life before. Cristina, an Argentinean woman with and from a large family has the incredible skill to make cooking for five thousand look like a breeze! I could never be in better hands, and I see how much they want to show their love and respect for Michael.

Ceci and her team from the University will be filming the ceremony and I am in regular contact with them to organise all kinds of practical tasks about this.

The next key person I contact is my friend Tania. I ask her if she will help to facilitate the ceremony. Whilst I have facilitation skills, this is not something that I want to be doing myself. I want a friend who is strong and capable enough for me to lean on at this time and Tania is the very best friend that I can think of for this job. She helps immediately and without question.

Unbelievably, I have only given myself two weeks to pull this ceremony together. What am I thinking? The sheer enormity of the task starts to hit me as the preparations begin. For the first weekend after our return, I have booked us into a hotel at Hong Kong

Disneyland, just thirty minutes' drive from our home, to attempt to ease some of the painful pressures of living in a home that is no longer a home. Diana is with her best friend, Susanne. Whilst they are playing and swimming, I arrange to meet up with Malou and Tania for a ceremony planning session at the hotel.

I collect Tania from the nearby MTR (Mass Transit Railway) station, driving barefoot with only my car keys, having just come from being with Diana and Malou at the poolside of the hotel, when I suddenly notice a police car behind me. The police ask me to stand outside the car and tell me that I am not allowed to be parked in this spot. They ask to see my driving licence, which is back in the hotel safe. They then show me that my car licence is one month out of date. I had absolutely no idea, as this hasn't been in the foreground in my mind! I can feel myself beginning to shake with fear and stress.

Thankfully, Tania arrives in this moment and helps me to explain to the police how I have just returned from my husband's funeral in the UK. Eventually, and to my significant relief, they let me off with a warning and I drive us back to the hotel, intensely aware of my vulnerability and of my limited control of practical matters.

Tania, Malou and I then focus on the tasks that face us for the ceremony. I have the broad ideas. I want to put beach mats on the sand in a semicircle and to open up a space for people to speak. Tania, my New Zealand friend and perfect choice as a facilitator, reminds me that some people might want to speak and that others will not, so it will be useful for us to create some structure. She suggests that we 'plant' some people to speak and to give readings so that they can prepare in advance, as well as leave some open spaces.

So it is that the ceremony takes shape. Tania and Elize, a friend and neighbour from Tong Fuk, suggest introducing the use of a 'talking stick', a wooden stick that Tania collects from the beach that can be passed to those who wish to speak, Elize having been initiated into their use through a Native Indian tribe in Canada. Tania suggests that we produce a service sheet. The thought of doing so at this late stage is totally overwhelming so I ask our friends Ed and Cheryl if they will create this as they have computer skills. They, like all our other friends, lend their support without question. Malou and my other friends already have the food, flowers and decoration planning underway and want only to check out any particular wishes that I might have.

There is one section in the ceremony that I want as a space for me. Only one image comes to mind and I discuss it openly with Tania and Malou for the first time. I want to go to buy a gold chain from a special jeweller that Debra introduced me to many years before, and I would like to remove my engagement and wedding rings in front of our friends as witnesses, in the same way as Michael and I originally put them onto each other's hands at our wedding. I would then like to place my rings alongside Michael's to wear on the gold chain around my neck.

My friends are visibly shocked. Malou starts to gently explain how, in her culture, it is traditional to be in mourning for quite some time after the funeral and to wear black. Tania tells me how people will be coming to pay their respects and might not know how to react if they suddenly start to see me taking off my wedding ring.

I feel completely taken aback and very upset. This is my space, my only space. Michael and I put on our wedding rings in front of our family and friends, and now I would like to honour our marriage contract and vows in this same way. We made a commitment to 'love, honour and cherish each other until death do us part'. We have each honoured all of our vows. I have loved Michael and supported him for so long, even to the extent of taking his body home to Scotland, and now I want to start to 'let go'. Yet, the very last thing that I want to do is to shock and upset my friends—the friends who are coming to show their last respects. I absolutely don't know what to do so I turn to Ceci and ask to meet with her.

In distress, I explain the problem to Ceci, who offers me a new word. She says, "Your marriage vows are completed."

The word 'completed' fits perfectly and is much better than 'ended'. As we talk, an idea emerges. I ask if Ceci might sit by my side in the ceremony and open up 'my space'. She would help to educate and explain to my friends what I want to do, so as to lessen potential feelings of shock and to prepare the audience for my actions, whilst also enabling me to have a space to honour my feelings and my desire to complete my wedding vows in this way. This act is far from intended to shock; rather, it is for me wonderful, loving, respectful and honest. Our wedding vows are completed. I know that Michael has died. I have walked with him every step of his dying until the very end. Ceci fully understands my desire for this ritual and lends me her full support to be by my side.

Later, Ceci asks, "How did you come up with this idea of running a memorial service on the beach?"

I answer, "To be honest, the inspiration for the memorial on the beach came from my heart. When I sat and reflected on Michael and what he means to me, this is the image that came to me—the beach, the semicircle, the community—and it was such a strong image that just came from my heart and my soul. It wasn't logical thinking. It was just very powerful and it never went away. I feel for me that it is an expression of love and tribute for Michael and it is also something that is resonating and important for me and for Diana."

This statement is so true: this decision is a creatively inspired, intuitive idea, and while it is incredibly important to me, I have not had any time to look at the practicalities. Indeed the sheer enormity of these hits me hard in the face as my original idea starts to be translated into reality in such a short time.

After the progress meeting, one new and considerable challenge faces me. It is now looking like more than one hundred people will attend the ceremony and, with the natural backdrop of the waves, however gentle these are, there is a strong probability that no one will be able to hear the proceedings. In addition to this, I am frightened that the local police might put a stop to a public gathering on a beach. My fear intensifies as I imagine this special intimate moment turning into an absolute nightmare. I simply hadn't thought all of these logistical issues through.

With the support of a friend, we speak with the Village Head. I then learn how he and his family want to offer us help and support, yet do not know how, as they have never before faced the death of an expatriate member of the local community in this way. Without question, he speaks with the lifeguards and the local community, and lends his support in protecting this event held at a time when the public beach is empty of tourists. I am so deeply grateful. As for the sound, the University of Hong Kong looks to see if we can hire equipment. In the end, it is our male friends in the village, especially Jörg with the support of JP, who take on this particular challenge and hook up powerful speakers.

One final step in the preparations is for me to prepare my own words. I choose to sit in The Gallery with a stack of white postcards and a refreshing glass of white wine to do so.

There is one other aspect to the preparations that I have not written of to date. One of the traditional rituals of paying respect to the deceased is to offer financial donations. Michael and I have been unable to work much over the past year, since the loss of his leg and then his subsequent surgeries. We are very short of money and living hand to mouth at this time. I have no idea what my future will bring and am very frightened by the financial pressures that face me. I have never in my life asked for charity. Yet, I make the difficult yet important decision to put pride to one side and to ask for what Diana and I really need at this time, which is financial support.

My close friends encourage and support me in this step and take the initiative to help Diana and me in this way. Having gently sought my permission, Joe contacts Michael's colleagues who offer generous donations. He and Steve also help me to contact two charitable organisations linked to Michael's professional bodies, which offer us financial assistance. Tom, a close friend and neighbour, coordinates local donations from friends in our community. I am so pleased that I make this decision as the financial support of others cushions us at this—the very worst—moment of our lives to date.

On the morning of Michael's beach ceremony, the whole village is quietly and respectfully busy. It is truly an awe-inspiring and incredible experience for me. Down on the beach, huge banana leaves and white flowers are being turned by Grace into incredible displays, worthy of any top designer flower shop. Malou, Stella, Cristina and Elize are covering plastic and wooden beach tables with white tablecloths, spreading out an array of decorations.

One of the many wonderful aspects of the morning is that most of the children from the village are down on the beach, collecting seashells for the displays, playing in the sand, and helping the parents with all the preparations. We have talked in advance about how to involve the children of the village and here they are. The photos of the morning show children on rocks, children running and playing. In my home, Diana and her friends are busy with Jenny rehearsing a dance that they have prepared for the ceremony. Our house is full of laughter, noise and organised chaos. All of our closest friends are busy doing something, each with individual roles, like an orchestra tuning up and preparing for a concert.

At the last minute, Terry has miraculously found a Hong Kong piper who arrives at the beach in his tracksuit and starts to practise. This is an amazing achievement and sight. Ronnie and other friends are gently strumming and tuning up their guitars. Jörg and Winnie's family dog, Lottie, walks on the sand and lies by the food table as she does at all village parties. Friends are social yet also quiet and reflective. The open expanse of sand allows people space to sit on rocks in silent contemplation looking out over the waves, as the children collect shells and preparations are taking place. The film crew arrives and the men of the village busy themselves with wires and technical issues. There are a few last-minute panics as we realise that we might not have enough lights and the call goes out for lanterns.

This whole experience is something totally incredible for me to be a part of. Whilst the original vision for this ceremony was mine, the actual occasion now has a life and energy all of its own—much bigger and much more amazing than anything that I could have imagined and of which I am now simply one of the parts.

Gradually more and more people arrive. Ceci has brought her family with her as well as her colleagues. It is lovely to meet them in this way. I go home to change. I wear black and white, just as I did in Scotland for Michael's funeral. When I return, the piper is wearing his kilt and welcomes guests arriving at the beach with 'Amazing Grace'. I am immediately transported back in my thoughts to our wedding day in February 1993 in the cold misty Bolton air.

Ceci interviews our friends:

> My generation and the previous generation don't talk about death or about anything that might be uncomfortable. The whole thing about Sandra and Michael that impressed me is that they were absolutely open. There was nothing that they wouldn't discuss. And I personally found that absolutely liberating. It has changed my whole attitude towards these subjects. We can sit and talk with Sandra now about Michael and what happened and what will happen. There are no tricky areas. It's all out there and it's just wonderful. It's taken the big scare out of it for me; it

really has. I'm much more receptive to new ideas although we are not planning on it just yet!

Barbara

Tong Fuk is a very sharing community and this ceremony for Michael has been a labour of love. It's a good feeling and it is very good for everyone to be in a community because we share happy and joyful as well as sad moments like this. During sad times such as this one, the support of the community really helps.

Malou

Death of course is an unfortunate event and, for me, this is an opportunity to show my support to Sandra because, for sure, it is a very difficult moment for her and this is a time that we can show her our love, our care and that she will never be alone; there are always people around her, especially at this time, to support her.

Stella

Today is very special for me. We always have very nice parties and very nice moments with Michael. And today, before I came here to prepare, I think about how nice it is for everyone to help, to give part of your heart to support somebody at this time. When you have someone whom you have loved and lost, you never say goodbye, you only say goodbye when there are no more feelings left in your heart. I think now that Michael is with us and that we did all of this nice job to support Sandra but also to say Michael is with us now.

Cristina

These words and actions, and those of all our friends present at Michael's ceremony, are selfless displays of love that illustrate the power of community, no less so given that they are shared by people of different cultures, nationalities and backgrounds. This is truly a lesson in love.

Gradually everyone sits down. Ed and Cheryl have produced the most beautiful service sheets that we hand out to all. I look out at the waves and allow myself to be present with all my emotions, knowing and trusting that I am held, like I have never been held before, by those around me.

Ronnie and Grace and other Filipino friends open with a guitar instrumental of 'You'll Never Walk Alone'. Elize, our South African friend, plays Loreena McKennitt's 'Dante's Prayer':

> Cast your eyes on the ocean
> Cast your soul to the sea

Diana and her friend Susanne wear matching yellow T-shirts, especially chosen and that they still love and wear today. There is a large rock by the edge of the sea that all the children climb. Diana moves freely with the other children between the group, the rocks, the beach and the sea. I watch the children as I listen to the waves. I open the ceremony by thanking everyone for being with us. I have invited Paddy to speak first and to open the sharing. Some of the many special words that Paddy says include:

> Whilst Sandra and Michael have always ensured that Diana is aware of what is happening, they have also always ensured that, as much as possible, she will have her normal existence as well, and that is hugely important.

Paddy then reads out a verse from Shakespeare's *The Tempest* on behalf of Jane and Leo who are in Beijing. Jane is English and Leo is Chinese.

> Our revels now are ended. These our actors,
> As I foretold you, were all spirits and
> Are melted into air, into thin air:
> And, like the baseless fabric of this vision,
> The cloud-capp'd towers, the gorgeous palaces,
> The solemn temples, the great globe itself,
> Ye all which it inherit, shall dissolve
> And, like this insubstantial pageant faded,
> Leave not a rack behind. We are such stuff
> As dreams are made on, and our little life
> Is rounded with a sleep.

> William Shakespeare
> *The Tempest*, Act IV, Scene i

Our good friend Boz, a New Zealander, speaks:

> I have the utmost respect for Michael. He was the most patient man and, for me, he really typifies a human being that knows how to think about other people in the midst of their own problems. I believe that as a human being, that really typifies maturity and he was a wonderful friend and I'll never forget him.

I then light a candle for Harold Crowter, as he is entering into the last days or weeks of his life, also now losing his battle with cancer. Harold has stood alongside Michael and me for so many years and offered the money for Michael's first heart surgery when our insurance company refused to pay. "Harold, I have already spoken with and written to you. We owe you so much and I light this candle in respect and in honour of you."

I ask my friend and colleague, Vivian, to read a verse that she had sent to me:

> Cancer is so limited...
> It cannot cripple love.
> It cannot shatter hope.
> It cannot corrode faith.
> It cannot eat away peace.
> It cannot destroy confidence.
> It cannot kill friendship.
> It cannot shut out memories.
> It cannot silence courage.
> It cannot reduce eternal life.
> It cannot quench the Spirit.

Anonymous
'What Cancer Cannot Do'

Accompanied by the acoustic guitars, we all sing 'Let It Be' by The Beatles.

> I wake up to the sound of music,
> Mother Mary comes to me.
> Speaking words of wisdom, let it be.

I have asked our close friend Edward to choose and read a poem:

When I am gone, release me, let me go
I have so many things to see and do
You must not tie yourself to me with tears
Be happy that I have had so many years

I gave you my love, you can only guess
How much you gave me in happiness
I thank you for the love each have shown
But now it is time I traveled on alone

So grieve a while for me, if grieve you must
Then let your grief be comforted by trust
It is only for a while that we must part
So bless the memories in your heart

I will not be far away, for life goes on
So if you need me, call and I will come
Though you can not see or touch me, I will be near
And if you listen with your heart, you will hear
All of my love around you soft and clear

Then, when you must come this way alone
I will greet you with a smile and a
'Welcome Home'

Mary Alice Ramish
'To Those Whom I Love and Those Who Love Me'

Choking back her tears, Cheryl reads a letter that she has written to Michael:

Dear Michael,

I want you to know that you have taught me so many precious life lessons. It is easy to say things like "You need to have faith and trust God when things go wrong." It all sounds wonderful, but I think that everyone knows that when it actually comes down to doing it, it's very hard.

Because of you and your example, however, I know that it's possible to face an impossible situation, one that you have no control over, surrender that to God and trust Him for the strength and then go on through the storm in peace. You did it. I saw you do it. I look at you and I see someone just like me, a human being, a normal person, the guy next door and yet what you did is something that even superheroes don't do.

Looking at some famous person who seems to be especially gifted with strength, it is easy for me to say, "Well of course so-and-so can do it, but not me."

But because you were so down-to-earth and because you stayed the gentle, quiet Michael that you always were, you've equipped a normal, everyday person like me with a confidence that life's challenges can be faced right up until the end in peace, hope and joy. I do believe that you have given me a treasure that no money can buy.

May the life that you lived continue to bless many and while I'm very sad that I won't see you for a while, I believe, like it says in your message to us, that we will meet again one day in Heaven and you will say to me, "Welcome Home." I love you Michael.

Our Australian friend, John, reads a message from an absent English friend, Clive:

I used to stand at the bus stop in Discovery Bay for the bus to Tung Chung, waiting for Michael to join me, hoping that we could be on the same bus and to be able to sit next to each other. We would chat away, really enjoying our time together, such good company, such a kind and considerate man. The bus journey was never long enough. We had so much to talk about and, most importantly, we would laugh together. Happy days.

We learn that Clive has made his own tribute to Michael:

I skipped up a mountain in the Lake District. 6 am. I started and at 7 am I was at the top—eight hundred metres—just me and a cloud with my prayers for Michael. My thoughts were about the good times that we have had—and they were good times—and I miss them very much. I said goodbye to Michael. He heard me.

Tania reads a message to Diana and me from another New Zealand friend, Lucinda, now living back in New Zealand:

Across the ocean though we may be, our shores are met across the sea today. I breathe in and I breathe out as the waves ebb and flow. We are connected here by more than physical presence. Our paths have crossed and we have leaned on each other as friends, influenced, moved and changed.

As I turn to the sea my spirit follows its power across the waves and I am standing beside you shoulder to shoulder—my soul sister. I feel that Michael is here with you today. His energy is here. He has loved you, moved and changed you forever, as he has all of us. His being has touched us all and, in essence, is carried forward, like ripples across the water. You are richer and more beautiful now, having shared Michael's life path. He is indeed a wonderful part of both you and Diana and we should celebrate that.

Tania hands me a crystal from Lucinda:

I offer you this crystal from my heart, chosen for its mystery and beauty. At first cool and heavy and aching with resignation, nature—our glorious Mother that cannot be denied—will claim it back into its folds and into the depth of her being. This is home, this great place of mystery, reckoning, beauty and peace.

Yet this stone is also chosen for its hidden depths, a piece of molten nature captured for a while passed to this earth. A soft warmth is within; at the core of its being is a kernel of energy and love and from this I know that all things are possible.

The stone may melt to sand in the mighty sea, transmute and change shape, but from it life springs forth in new ways with all its new possibilities. Though it may roll and tumble awhile in the tide at nature's behest, as you may feel that you are, my wish is that you take the solace stone into your hands now, feel its energy and slowly, gently shift that energy in your own special way into a new beginning, new possibilities, a new life filled with love and wisdom.

Please cast this stone and remember Michael. Remember your love, remember who you are, your essence and feel who you will be. Let the sea wash the stone away and uplift your spirit and take the stone's essence with you in love energy. I see your spirit shining brightly with pure energy. Smile and know that there is love and peace within.

From across this ocean, I send you all my love.
Your soul sister,
Lucinda

I light a candle to send my love to Colin Lewin, my wish for him to remain cancer-free after his chemotherapy treatment, and my thanks for his being at our side in Scotland for Michael's funeral and at so many times in our recent lives: "Colin, this candle is sent with deep love and deep gratitude to you."

Grace sings a beautiful song, strumming along to her guitar.

You remember me, when the soft wind blows,
Upon the waves of Tong Fuk.
With its clear blue skies
And where eagle flies
As we walk in sands of gold.

The piper pipes as we all sing 'Amazing Grace'. Diana and her close friends—Susanne, Sabrina, Tiara and Noel—sing and perform the special dance that she has selected and rehearsed with Jenny as her tribute to her dad, to the tune of 'Gotta Go My Own Way'.

Ceci, who has been sitting by my side through the ceremony, speaks:

Confucius has a saying that if you don't know about life, you don't talk about death. But in fact, I think that the reverse is true: when we experience the death of Michael, which is sad, which is a loss, with the verses, the prayers, the dance, the songs, the poems, all of them are so revealing. They give us inspiration about what a life is about, about his spirit to fight and his jokes and his commitment to changing the world, to finding solutions.

I don't know Michael at all. I learned of him through a conversation with Sandra, and Sandra has such enormous spirit, which amazed me. During this conversation, she learned how there was so much that she could do during these last, most precious days with him in her life.

At this time, she, Michael and Diana shared what was important in their lives with each other, when they expressed and talked about their love for each other, of forgiveness, of appreciation, when they shared a special bottle of wine with memories of their wedding anniversary and when Michael shared some words of wisdom for life with Diana.

As Sandra said, I am running a project on death education. A problem with society today is that death is such a taboo; we don't talk about it. If we don't talk about it then we don't think about it. For the Chinese, it is worse; if we think about it then we think that it will bring bad luck. As we don't prepare and as we don't think about it, when death comes, it always comes too suddenly. It always comes too early. Because of lack of preparation, there are a lot of things that we feel, "Oh, I should have done that before he or she died," and there is a lot of guilt left behind with prolonged grief.

There it is absolutely important, as in the case of Sandra, she used fully the last few days of Michael's life to complete her relationship and to express their love for each other and made this a beautiful love story that is completed, that is wrapped up in a beautiful ribbon and left stored in her heart.

There is a Taoist ritual in Chinese funerals that involves the breaking of a comb. In Chinese rituals, the husband combs the hair of his wife every morning, ideally. In the funeral, the wife of the husband who has died is asked to break the comb, to break it into two halves so as to symbolise the fact that the husband will no longer be able to comb the hair of this wife and the wife will have to move on.

So, I found a plastic comb that cannot be broken and I am giving this as a gift to Sandra. Her love for Michael will always be there and this comb, like the love that Michael gave her, will always stay with her.

My vision for this ceremony has all been a tribute to Michael, yet within it, I have also created space for me to make my personal tribute. In it I choose to honour the completion of our marriage.

Michael, on the 6th February 1993, we made our wedding vows to each other: for better, for worse, for richer, for poorer, in sickness and health until death do us part. Neither of us knew then just how much we would be tested on every single one of those vows to the extreme.

And yet, through all these tests, and I don't know how, but somehow we each found a way to honour every single vow. I am so proud of that. I consider that a tribute to us both and a great act of love. Our marriage was a true foundation of love and partnership, out of which Diana was created and through Diana and through me, our love will live on. I love you. I'll always love you. And yet, in the words of the song of the children, I've also now 'gotta go my own way' even though I don't know how.

For me, this ceremony is about trying to begin to let go, having taken you home to Scotland, which was my vow that I made to you and now to come back to our home. I wanted a way, and asked for Cecilia's support to find a way for me to begin to let go, not to say goodbye but to complete, because the circle of our wedding vows is completed.

With Cecilia's help, I went to my friend Debra's favourite jewellers and I bought a very strong gold chain to put Michael's and my wedding rings and my engagement ring on to. None of you were present when we got married but there was a wonderful part in the service where Michael put my ring on the wrong finger by accident and the best man suddenly asked if anyone had any butter.

What Cecilia is going to do now, is to support me in completing our wedding vows. Our marriage has come full circle. I honour you Michael, I love you and I now also begin to let go and to recognise the completion of our marriage.

After the removal of my rings I am alone, throwing the special crystal from Lucinda into the sea and staring out at the ocean, listening to the music dedicated to me by Michael: The Flaming Lips' 'Do you Realize??'.

As I turn my attention back to the group, something totally unplanned has happened: all our friends are holding hands in a large circle listening to the music with one space left for me. The group has taken its own shape. I hold Ceci's hand on my right and that of Diana's teacher, Tom, on my left. I soak in the strength of our friends. It is a deeply empowering moment, like when a starving child finally takes in some food. I also later learn something else: Tom has the same birth date as Michael—22nd March.

A coincidence? My trusty Collins Dictionary definition of 'coincidence' is: 'A chance occurrence of events remarkable either for being simultaneous or for apparently being connected.'

I experience such instances as kind of 'larger than life' and I always remember someone once saying how 'coincidences are God's way of remaining hidden.'

The Swiss psychologist Carl Gustav Jung writes of 'meaningful coincidences' and of the idea of synchronicity. The idea of synchronicity is that the conceptual relationship of minds, defined as the relationship between ideas, is intricately structured in its own logical way and gives rise to relationships that are not causal in nature. These relationships can manifest themselves as simultaneous occurrences that are meaningfully related—the cause and the effect occur together. One of Jung's quotes on synchronicity is from Through the Looking Glass by Lewis Carroll, in which the White Queen says to Alice, "It's a poor sort of memory that only works backwards." In this moment of poignant coincidence I feel Michael's presence with me.

The Early Days without Michael
October 2007—March 2008

I'll sail this ship alone
Between the pain and the pleasure

The Beautiful South
'I'll Sail This Ship Alone'

THE GRIEVING PROCESS

The positive emotions and support from Michael's ceremony boost me
for the first few weeks afterwards. I feel buoyed up on this amazing
experience. Then gradually, the painful awareness of the reality of my
situation and deep existential feelings of loss seep in.

After Michael's funeral and ceremony, our family and friends
return to their own lives as before. They move on. This is natural. This
is normal. For me, however, now begins the real pain, the real 'letting
go', and the real grieving. Now I am out on the open seas, cast adrift.

Ceci introduces me to a crisis-counselling model by Dr. Grace
Christ, a social work professor in Columbia University, generated
through her work with families who lost loved ones in 9/11. She
reminds me that everyone has his own pace of grieving and suggests
that I might use this model as a framework for tracking the path of
my own grief.

Dr. Christ's work shows that a state of 'trauma' was extremely
intense in year one, strongly intense in year two, moderately intense
in year three, and became more intermittent in year four. 'Grief and
mourning' were strongly intense in year one, extremely intense in
year two and intermittent in years three and four.

Stop for a moment as you read and listen to her findings again.

When we support family and friends with bereavement, is this kind of four-year timescale for trauma something that we think about? The 'normal' focus of community grieving, certainly in my experience, is around the funeral. We pay our respects and then we go home. Where I grew up, in fact, we never spoke much in my family when people died, even when we were very close to these people. Of course, not all bereavement is associated with the same level of 'trauma' as that of these grieving 9/11 families. Nonetheless, I see this model as a valuable one. Diana and I have now lived with trauma for eight to ten years, facing Michael's potential dying many times before it happened. His death, while not surprising, is nonetheless shocking.

According to *Webster's Dictionary*, the word 'trauma' comes from the Greek for 'wound' or 'injury'. Significantly, one of the many valuable lessons Ceci teaches is to think of myself as having an 'invisible disability'. It is both an emotional and physical disability that others cannot see.

Having shared this message with my new friend Sharon whose husband also died recently, she replies:

> I totally agree with the disability context you mentioned. People do not realise that I am living life from a totally different perspective (with no joy and happiness for now—just 'elderly' reflection and gratefulness). They forget that I am so sad, because I act sooooooooooooooooooooooo 'normal'—naturally positive and smiley, because I am not harping on and reminding people of how different my whole being is, to where they are in their lives.
>
> When people ask, "How is it going?", I know they are referring to the day-to-day practical running of my life, as opposed to referring to the insane mental turmoil my mind and body grapples with daily!

There is so much to learn here, not only for the bereaved, but also for the families and friends who seek to support us. It is really striking to me that the average person is not trained in any way in understanding death and dying when we are all trained in so many other things.

When (not 'if'!) we face bereavement, our own as well as others', we have no frame of reference, unless, like me, we are incredibly fortunate to find a teacher along the way. A key purpose in my writing this book is to encourage us to be open in sharing such wisdom as there is in our communities—what works and what doesn't.

PROFESSIONAL SUPPORT

'Trauma management' is an area of medical expertise that most of us don't have within our immediate skills-set. For me, one of the lynchpins in my support network is my relationship with my GP. Wherever I have lived in the world, I have quickly established a link with a local GP with whom I feel comfortable to discuss emotional as well as physical issues.

Throughout Michael's illness, I remain in regular contact with my GP in Hong Kong to monitor my own emotional and physical health. In the extremely traumatic year leading up to Michael's death, we both decide it might be helpful for me to start to take anti-depressants as a way of balancing my emotional stability. This was a proactive decision that really helped me. My GP chose a fairly low dose of anti-depressant, not wanting to numb my emotions so much that I would not have access to them during my grieving. I see her as a critical part of my support network in that she is able to assess my health and well-being from a medical perspective, which my friends and family are simply not equipped to do.

I have also had the amazing privilege of being able to lean on Ceci for support. It is important for me to share my learning from Ceci with you so that we can all benefit from having her by our side. Through Ceci, I have been introduced to Dr. Robert A. Neimeyer, another global expert in death education and counselling. I now understand that there is a significant body of specialist research into this topic and that grief is a known process. Awareness of these frameworks lends me support: I realise that I am not alone or unusual; I also know that there are professionals I can turn to for support.

Dr. Therese A. Rando, whose seminar in 'Traumatic Bereavement' I attended in Hong Kong in April 2009, is clear that there is no right answer for grieving and that what is supportive to one person might cause further pain to another: 'One man's meat is another man's poison.'

Dr. Robert A. Neimeyer in his book, *Lessons of Loss*, advises, 'You yourself are probably the best gauge as to whether reaching out—to your minister, your doctor, a support group, or a mental health professional—could help you move forward with your own grieving and gradual reorganisation. Though we must all attempt to find meaning in our losses and in our continuing lives, there is no reason that we must do so heroically, without the support, advice, and tangible assistance of others.'

He further advises that although there is nothing "abnormal" about the pain, loneliness and disruption that accompany bereavement, there are some conditions under which you may owe it to yourself and others to reach out to the professional or lay helpers in your environment. While the decision will be personal for each griever, you should seriously consider talking to someone about your grief symptoms if you experience any of the following conditions:

> **Substantial guilt**, about things other than the actions you took or did not take at the time of a loved one's death.

> **Suicidal thoughts**, which go beyond a passive wish that you would be 'better off dead' or could reunite with your loved one.

Extreme hopelessness, a sense that no matter how hard you try, you will never be able to recover a life worth living.

Prolonged agitation or depression, a feeling of being 'keyed up' or 'slowed down' that persists over a period of months.

Physical symptoms, such as stabbing chest pain or substantial weight loss that could pose a threat to your physical well-being.

Uncontrolled rage that estranges friends and loved ones or leaves you 'plotting revenge' for your loss.

Persistent functional impairment in your ability to hold a job, or accomplish routine tasks required for daily living.

Substance abuse, relying heavily on drugs or alcohol to banish the pain of loss.'

He concludes that '[w]hile any of these conditions may be a temporary feature of normal bereavement, their continued presence is cause for concern and deserves attention by someone beyond the informal support figures in your life.'

My personal journey definitely involves the support of professionals as well as that of family, friends and community.

LEARNING TO COPE AFTER MICHAEL'S DEATH

In the seconds and days, weeks and months following Michael's death, I naturally, without conscious deliberation, draw on my trusty, well-honed skills of living moment to moment. It is a very simple truth that other actions, such as looking ahead or planning for the future, are so overwhelming that I don't know how else to get through each day.

One of the acutely painful experiences for me after Michael's death is the absence of his voice. Throughout the whole of our married life, Michael and I speak every day, often several times a day. During Michael's dying, Ceci suggests that I record his voice and I don't get my act together with the technology. I so wish that I had, as it is the absence of his voice and his physical absence that hurt me such a great deal, especially in these early days. We do have the voice recording from his mobile phone, which I play and listen to over and over.

Another immediate source of acute pain for me is the fact that my 'home', the home that I built with Michael, no longer feels like home. My one place of respite is now not. There is nothing in the immediate short-term that I am able to do to change this experience.

In the early months following Michael's death, my friend Sally takes the lead role in a play called *The Rabbit Hole*, performed in the Academy for Performing Arts in Hong Kong. I invite Ceci and her niece to watch the play with me. Ceci has just returned from supporting victims of the earthquakes in Sichuan and is so completely exhausted that she has lost her voice. Her presence at this time grounds me in the wider global context of my own grief. Having known for sure my personal pain, I find it overwhelming to imagine the pain of wide scale grief and loss, much less having to think how to help people with this.

The Rabbit Hole enacts the story of a married couple, Becca and Howie, whose young son Danny has died. The play speaks to me on so many levels.

A particularly striking aspect for me is the relationship that the couple has with their home. One parent wants to immediately get rid of all their son's belongings, as the pain of seeing them is too hard to bear.

Becca explains to her husband how she wants to sell the house: "He's everywhere, Howie. Everywhere I look, I still see Danny."

He, on the other hand, feels angry that she has taken Danny's paintings off the wall and put them away in a box, and removed his clothes and shoes. When she accidentally records over a childhood video of Danny, he blames her for doing it on purpose.

"You have to stop erasing him! You have to stop it!"

Becca replies, "Do you really not know me, Howie? Do you really not know how utterly impossible that would be? To erase him? No matter how many things I give to charity or how many art projects I box up, do you really think I don't see him every second of every day?"

My initial reaction at our home is the same as Becca's. It is so painful for me to see not only Michael's personal possessions but all of our possessions—everything that we have built together as a couple—that I want to destroy everything, to throw things away, to remove everything so that I don't have to look at and be with them anymore. I totally empathise with bereaved spouses who choose to leave their home and move to a new one. I long to do so rather than to bear this pain, especially in the one place that has been my source of respite and comfort.

Diana, like Howie in the play, has the exact opposite response: the desire for everything to remain exactly the same forever, as it is so acutely painful to let anything go. To hold on to everything in the home is to hold onto the loved one. She cries and complains when I even speak of making small changes at home, like moving a photo on the wall.

There is one occasion when I remove an old chair that Michael used to sit on so that I can create a sense of space in the living room. The chair is falling apart anyway as we have had it for many years. We remove the chair when Diana is at school and I am clearing the house.

When Diana returns, I can only describe her emotional state as absolutely grief-stricken. She bursts into inconsolable floods of tears and is furious with me. The removal of 'Michael's chair' cushions me from falling off the sheer cliff of grief and pushes Diana over the edge. From this moment on, I never remove any item from the home without involving Diana in the process. I determine to seek to manage our shared grief process in a way that is caring for—and supportive of—each other.

As I watch the play, I see the daily reality that Diana and I are living enacted in front of my eyes. It would be wonderful to be able to report that Diana and I manage to find a place of balance, yet this would not be the truth. Like the characters in the play, there is a communication void between Diana and me as our instinctual responses to the agonising pain of loss move in equal and opposite directions.

Becca says to her husband, "But just let me say, Howie, that I am mourning as much as you are. And my grief is just as real and awful as yours ... You're not in a better place than I am, you're just in a different place. And that sucks that we can't be there for each other right now, but that's just the way it is."

As I watch the play, I see that I am no longer in the normal parental role of supporting my daughter. Instead, we are each walking around our home in our own separate pool of grief.

One aspect of my learning here is that I am not best equipped at this stage in my life to support Diana alone, so I turn to Alicia, the child psychologist who works with play therapy. Still today, two years later, Diana meets with Alicia on a regular basis. I want Diana to know that there are other adults on whom she can lean for support with different thoughts, feelings and views from mine.

I focus my attention on small, achievable tasks, one of which is to gradually get Diana back to school. She has always loved school, yet, for the first time ever, does not want to go back. Her teacher, Jim, supports her return carefully, for example, with flexible homework demands.

Soon after her return it is time for her next school camp in Pui O. At this stage my main contact with the outside world is with Diana's school, so helping out again on camp flows naturally from this process and offers me support, company and fresh air outside of home.

It is here that I start to notice another aspect of my grieving that continues to manifest for about eighteen months. There are several occasions—remarkable not only for me but also for those present with me—when I have been ambling along through my day, with all looking normal from the outside, when suddenly and without warning someone will say or do something and I burst into tears—deep-flowing, unstoppable tears. I feel considerable relief when I witness these same sudden outbursts from the characters in *The Rabbit Hole*!

The first time that this happens is on school camp, when I take a child to the clinic to get stitches after she gashes her foot open on a rock. I go alone to support her. In so doing, I completely overestimate my own emotional strength, and when I return to camp, I burst into tears. The last time that I set foot in a hospital was when Michael died.

Despite this episode, it is wonderful to be away on school camp again. Like an escape, it provides me with nourishment and a clear focus. I am part of a team; I feel the support of those around me. Like being in my sister's home, it is nice to cushion myself around the campfire for a while, although then I have to return home, and that return is so painful. Any small 'ending' for me evokes the acute pain of the ultimate 'ending'. Small 'endings' are in themselves sheer agony as the pain and anger is so raw, each one is like a small 'death' that I must move through.

After school camp, with Diana settled back into her class, I have another major concern looming so large that I cannot escape it, although I long to run. I have been experiencing rectal bleeding and I feel absolutely terrified about this. What if something happens to me? Who will Diana have then? This is a medical problem that has occurred on and off since my pregnancy.

After a series of tests, surgical intervention is recommended and I decide to go ahead with it, whilst feeling terrified about going under anaesthetic in case I do not wake up again.

In preparing for the surgery, I also put other arrangements in place. I speak with my sister Ali and with Valerie to ask if they will care for Diana in the event of my death. They agree, so I write up my new will. I speak with Paddy and Barbara to ask them if they are okay to be on hand to provide contingency emergency support here in Hong Kong. They are. I cannot believe that I am doing this, and I act as if in a dream. I explain gently to Diana that my surgery does not entail major risks like Daddy's did. She listens carefully and nods. She hugs me.

The surgery is practical and successful: I don't have cancer. The bleeding was brought on through stress. I recover quickly and am deeply grateful for friends who stand by me at this time, including Ceci and another new friend she introduces to me, Justina, whose husband, TP, sadly passed away on the same day as Michael.

Notwithstanding the successful outcome of the surgery, I constantly feel absolutely exhausted. I fall asleep often yet continue to have dark rims under my eyes. I notice how I sigh a lot. Eighteen months later, I decide to take a full hormone test as part of a general health check. We find out that I am suffering from hypothyroidism, which means that my thyroid is significantly underperforming. All the same symptoms that my GP and I have been attributing to grief are directly impacted by this condition. A few months into taking thyroxin tablets, I experience a notable shift in my energy levels.

I share this as important learning in not making assumptions about grief symptoms. I do not know how long I had battled with this condition yet the evident physical changes in me now suggest that I might have been doing so for a long time.

My surgery reminds me of my own physical health, to which I have given precious little attention whilst caring for Michael. From this time onwards I move this to the top of my priority list. I swim. I've joined a new gym. I continue with regular medical checks. I know that early detection can help with many illnesses and I see taking care of myself as a primary responsibility in my role as a mother. I'm not going to mess around with health—mine or that of others.

FACING A MOUNTAIN OF TASKS

In addition to the unexpected health issues, there are so many expected issues that I don't know where to even start talking about them. I have never, ever before faced such a mountainous task list. To help myself to feel any semblance of control, which I don't actually have, I separate the tasks in my mind into five broad categories: legal, financial, medical, house-sorting and administrative.

The one important thing to remember about all the many tasks in each of these categories is that I absolutely don't want to do any of them. These are all boring, tedious, time-consuming, emotional and expensive tasks that are only in my life because Michael has died. I don't want to do any of these tasks but I know that I have to. From the first day onwards, I decide to give space to my feelings and emotions. I leave the mountain to one side and tackle one task at a time, stopping when I have had too much or become too tired.

At first, I feel a lot of panic with this approach. What about all the things that are not getting done? I shut that pressure off. My choice of which task to address each day is determined quite simply by which is the most urgent. Often they have become so critical that there is no mistaking the need to address them!

When I feel tired, I stop and rest. Sometimes I sleep for the whole afternoon. I give in to my emotions. I allow them the space that they need. My will to fight is very low. I'm unsure if this is simply because we have been fighting so very hard for so many years.

With the wonderful benefit of hindsight, I can now see that, even with allowing my emotional space, my expectations regarding timescales for the accomplishment of tasks were completely and utterly unrealistic. Each task, however simple, drains me of energy.

I am in the very fortunate position of having a close family friend, Stephen, as my lawyer. He took over our legal affairs just before Michael died and has looked after us in so many ways that he is one of the many friends whom I shall never really know how to thank enough. I now know that three years is most probably a realistic timescale for all the different legal issues that I have faced. 20 months after Michael's death I faced new, unexpected legal problems when I sought to transfer his mortgage into my name. My advice to others is that dealing with lawyers—who are not family and friends—can be very stressful and it is important not to underestimate the legal costs involved. If it is possible to put aside savings to help with legal costs and to choose a lawyer whom you know well, then this could really help.

Financial matters easily become frightening for me. There are many reasons for this. One is that, in our marriage, Michael took more of a lead on such matters. A second is that I grew up in a family in which the message was very clear: there is never enough money. Lack of money is inbred as a frightening concept. This deep message still affects me, even though I have consistently worked and earned money since leaving home. A third is the reality of having to become the sole breadwinner whilst feeling so exhausted that I wonder if I shall ever work again.

Although frightened, I decide to 'feel the fear and do it anyway', making a clear decision to take three months off before returning to work. Earlier in the year I had approached the principal of Lantau International School to let him know of Michael's worsening condition. I explained to him that I did not know how long this situation would last. The principal very kindly assured me that Diana would finish the school year regardless of my financial distress. His support included waiving the school fees for me for a few months. I am deeply grateful to him for this.

I also decide to lean on the financial gifts to us that generous friends have made. Michael and I do both have some life insurance and pension provision in place. Michael's life insurance monies do not come through, however, until over a year after his death. Pension monies trickle through more gradually.

I talk about my financial fears and need for education with my friend Kate who originally trained as an accountant and who is knowledgeable in this field. I also turn to Suze Orman's books. One of the key messages that I take from these is the need for me to 'get real'. I decide to create a spreadsheet on which I shall track all my income and expenditure as they arise so that I know exactly what my financial reality looks like. This spreadsheet becomes an incredibly valuable tool that I continue to use. Each time a bill arrives in the house, I read it, pay it and, before I file it away, I enter it onto my spreadsheet. This gradually becomes a habitual task.

Another person whom I confide in about my fears and my new learning is my friend Caroline, now living in the UK. She speaks with her dad, Robert, for whom finance and investment is a hobby that he loves and has always taught his family about. Robert steps alongside me as a friend and has, to this date, supported me as if I were his own daughter. I talk through all my financial issues with him and he sends me newspaper clippings and writes out easy-to-read information sheets in order to educate me.

Robert explains how he has helped another widow to handle financial affairs, and questions why there is such an evident gap with regard to the teaching of financial matters in our global education systems.

I have so much to thank Robert for. Two years down the line, I am much better informed than I was about financial matters and also feel somewhat calmer about these, seeing them more from a practical, less emotional perspective.

I have not mentioned tasks relating to medical insurance claims before in this book. Throughout all the years of living with Michael's cancer, one of my key, ongoing and time-consuming tasks has been to file all the medical claims and to liaise with our insurance company. After all the problems we faced with medical insurance when Michael was first diagnosed with cancer, we successfully ended up with a named contact person in the UK offices of our insurers with whom I was constantly in telephone contact from corners of various hospitals and car parks. This huge task gradually diminishes in the months following Michael's death.

With regard to house-sorting, the highly emotional experience of removing Michael's chair taught me that this needs to be a slow, delicate process to take good care of my emotions and Diana's. Each time that I do clear something, I feel immediately exhausted. I decide to take one part of the house to slowly clear and then repaint. One large section of our home office contains all of Michael's work books—he has a well-ordered library. I speak with Michael's friend and colleague, Colin, who knows that another friend, James, is in the process of setting up his own business library. I know James, his wife Winnie and their family very well and I cannot think of a better home for Michael's books. James comes to our home to help me sort out the books. Winnie arranges for some stickers to be printed 'In Memory of Michael' to put inside his books. Diana and I later go to James's office and stick the labels inside the books together. This is a special and memorable experience.

This is just one of many similar tasks. I can honestly say that two years later, whilst I have worked steadily at them, there are many still outstanding. In one way, I feel amazed by the length of time that all of this is taking, and in another, I recognise just how very important it is to allow this process of change to unfold at its own emotional pace. I don't want to force or push this as I face quite enough pressures as it is.

As for the administrative tasks, I can barely even bring myself to write about these. Imagine all the typical chores that fill up each day, multiply them ten-fold and then picture doing them all. To me, this is an unbearable thought, which is why so many non-urgent administrative tasks remain unfinished still.

Please remember as you read about my sense of 'realistic timescales' that I live in a country where I don't have family around to support me but can afford help. I employ Jenny and her husband Dwight to support our family. Whilst I go out to earn the income, they help me to look after Diana, do all the household tasks and look after our pets. I know, for sure, that I would be absolutely nowhere near as task-focused as I have been able to be without their help. This is also emotional help, as Jenny and Dwight live with us as family, so I have a constant presence of other adults around me that I absolutely lean on.

One of the many immeasurable sources of support in our life is Diana's best friends and their parents. Diana has a small group of loyal, close friends whom she loves like sisters and from whom she is increasingly inseparable, both since the loss of her father and also as the girls now move into their teenage years.

My human resources consultancy work involves me travelling away from home to residential events, which I typically run every couple of months. I am often required to live in hotels, not only in Hong Kong, but also across Asia—in Singapore, Thailand or China—for up to a week at a time.

After taking three months out of work and leaning on the financial support of family and friends, my first return to delivering a residential Management Development Centre is stressful. In addition, facing separation from Diana for the first time after Michael's death is an emotional wrench. Separation is often a process that I attempt to navigate with a great deal of love and care, and never more so than in this case.

I talk with Diana a lot before this residential event, allowing her time and space to make choices in how she wants to manage this to best support herself. She does not want to live at home just with Jenny and Dwight, so we ask her best friend Susanne's mum, Malou, if she might stay with them whilst I am away. They live in the house just opposite ours. Malou and her husband JP, as always, offer immediate and unconditional support. Diana then starts to feel excited about my trip as she gets to spend a few days sleeping over with her best friend.

One other idea from Diana is that we will each select one special item for the other person to have by their side to hold and cuddle at any time whilst the other is away. I give Diana a soft toy rabbit that I have had since I was one year old, which comes with a family story of my having left him in a rhubarb patch as a child. This is how he came to be known as 'Floppy Ears' as his ears became floppy when my parents hung him out on the washing line to dry! She gives me the soft blue teddy bear that she put by her dad's side when he died.

We now carry forward this same ritual on every trip when we are apart from each other and it really helps. I now have different objects that I travel with, such as cuddly toys or a homemade badge with Diana's photo. Diana sometimes likes me to leave behind items of clothing that she can wrap herself in and smell me.

This arrangement works so well for Diana on this first trip that her separation anxiety—along with mine—is easing and it is now less important to put so much structure in place in advance. Diana is now comfortable with spending time in our home when I am away, knowing that she can also sleep over with any of her friends if she wants to. My gratitude for my friends who support these kinds of ongoing practical arrangements without question or concern will never cease. We simply could not do this without them and it is they who continue to gradually ease the healing process for Diana and me.

In giving so much attention to supporting Diana through these early work transitions, I still pay comparatively less attention to myself. Ceci says, "You are seeking to be a perfect mother to the extent of compromising your own needs." This pattern of behaviour is a familiar one to me. It is only once I have put my support framework in place for Diana that I am able to relax, knowing that she is cocooned in the warmth of her friends with whom she cuddles up in bed at night. I, on the other hand, sleep alone in hotel bedrooms. I don't cope so well with this and am grateful for the company of my colleagues. I also take sleeping tablets when necessary to help ensure that I get the sleep that I need.

Now, two years on from this experience, Diana and I separate from each other with much greater ease and fluidity of movement.

THE POWER OF COMMUNITY

Our family story clearly illustrates what it is to live in a caring, multicultural community. I open a clip that Charles has sent to me from YouTube of a song called 'Stand by Me', as part of a documentary film called *Playing for Change*. The introduction goes:

This song says, no matter who you are, no matter where you go in your life, at some point, you are going to need somebody to stand by you.

Roger Ridley in Santa Monica, California
Playing for Change

The video clips feature artistes in different parts of the world singing this song. I feel goose bumps as I listen to the music knowing how important it is for me that Charles sends me this clip at this time, when I have spent the past ten years living with the incredible experience of a multinational community standing by me and by each other, sharing happiness and tears like one large, caring, loving and supportive family. To quote my Argentinean friend, Cristina: 'This is people living without mask.'

The expatriate community that Sandra lives in is also extraordinary. It is composed of people from all over the world and they care for each other like brothers and sisters. After the memorial on the beach, they gathered in Sandra's home and shared life wisdom generated in the process of witnessing Michael's illness and death. Michael lived his life to the fullest and served as a role model of optimism and resilience even through his journey of disability and death.

Professor Cecilia Chan
In Celebration of Life

I imagine the power and strength of a global community finding ways to stand by each other with love, care, concern and peace, sharing the laughter and the tears in life. In such a world, the path of growth, the lessons from living and dying do not only have to lie in the hands of trained professionals, although they continue to have an integral and important role to play.

No I won't be afraid, no I won't shed one tear
Just as long as you people come and stand by me.

Grandpa Elliot in New Orleans, Louisiana
Playing for Change

COMMUNICATION

Despite living in, and feeling, the absolute, unconditional support of our community, I still experience problems knowing how best to communicate with others.

In the early weeks following Michael's death, I stay at home a lot and curl up. My main contact, as I have already mentioned, is with Diana's teachers, who have also become my friends, and with the close friends who have been by my side the whole time.

Looking back at my friend Sharon's e-mail when we are talking about Ceci's advice to think of bereaved people as having an 'invisible disability', I see that I have consistently spoken honestly and openly about what is going on for me, about my feelings and emotions. In so doing, I have taken considerable care also to think about the impact on the people I am speaking to. I have sought to be authentic whilst undergoing extremely traumatic experiences, which others naturally do not wish for in their lives. This has not been easy to achieve but has proved to have somewhat of a transformational role in my own life and in the lives of my family, friends, colleagues and community.

As the years pass and our friends talk of the experience of living in the community with our family, one of the things that strikes them most is how consistently open we are in sharing our experience and how different this is for them, having mostly grown up in cultures where cancer and dying are not subjects that are talked about at all.

To quote Paddy:

> But the first thing that I have to say is that, above all, what has struck me about this community and about Sandra and Michael's attitude to this incredibly demanding process is the openness and inclusiveness and the manner in which everybody has been willingly and helpfully and supportively involved.
>
> I don't know about many of the communities from which we all come. I do know that we come from a hugely different variety of communities, but certainly where we come from, Barbara and I, it's the very antithesis of the norm in the sense that normally the curtains come down, the doors close and it becomes internal and people are very sensitive about appearing to intrude, although they'd love to help. Not so here.
>
> One of the biggest things I've learned is that Sandra and

> Michael went out into the community, explained their position, looked for guidance and advice, received an enormous amount of information, guidance, support and advice and it all made it, I think, a very, very healthy exercise. And certainly that's the number one colossal message from me—the openness and inclusiveness is hugely important.

I most certainly hadn't set out with a structured project to openly communicate with others; rather I flowed with an inner drive, desire and intention of living my life side-by-side with others.

Without doubt, this has been a humbling and amazing experience. I cannot help but wish now to influence change in places where the norm is more of violence than of love.

Yet even within such an incredible, supportive community there continue to be communication challenges. On my way back to Hong Kong after Michael's funeral, I unexpectedly bump into one of Michael's colleagues at Heathrow Airport in London.

He asks, "How's it going?"

I reply, "I'm just returning from Michael's funeral."

He looks very uncomfortable and asks, "Apart from Michael, how are things going?"

I stare at him with a blank expression, completely incapable of knowing how to take this conversation further.

This snippet of conversation illustrates so poignantly the challenges that exist in communicating about death and dying, all the more so when multicultural differences also come into play. The colleague at Heathrow Airport is Hong Kong Chinese and in that culture, it is considered taboo and very unlucky to talk about death.

Our Hong Kong Chinese friend, Tong, says:

> So it's really, really amazing to have friends here for such sharing; it's also the first time I have come across such a sharing of death. People are always talking about 'vision' and they will make many strategies to achieve the vision. If a vision is so important in one's life, maybe we can take death as the ultimate vision for us. If so, not many people have strategies or planning or whatever management to achieve such a last vision of life.

If we don't even talk easily about the subject of death and dying, then how can we begin to create more sophisticated communication tools? I see it as of vital importance to raise this question so that we can build on current and future research to guide us in how best to communicate.

During the first year or so of my own grieving, I refer consistently to living in the 'here and now'. As such, I find broad, general questions like "How's it going?" to be completely overwhelming. I am better able to absorb, and am even comforted by more specific opening questions, such as "How's it going for you today?" or "How are you doing today?" The focus of the word 'today' enables me to respond honestly and openly from the 'here and now'.

Many people say how they don't want to speak about such matters because they 'don't know what to say'. In my experience, the knowledge of someone's presence is deeply comforting. It is the presence of my friends, much more than what they say, that has been consistently supportive to me. I would encourage people to worry less about what they say and recognise how valuable it is for friends and family to feel your presence—even through short messages and e-mails.

Others want to offer help and support but are genuinely unsure how to do so.

Robert A. Neimeyer in his book, *Lessons of Loss: A Guide to Coping*, includes the following table of guidance on supporting a mourner:

Do's and Don'ts when Reaching Out to a Mourner

Don't	Don't
Force the mourner into a role, by saying: "You're doing so well." Allow the mourner to have troubling feelings without the sense of letting you down.	**Open the door to communication**. If you aren't sure what to say, ask, "How are you feeling today?" or "I've been thinking about you. How is it going?"

Don't	Don't
Tell the mourner what he or she 'should' do. At best, this reinforces the mourner's sense of incompetence, and at worst, your advice can be "'off target'" completely.	**Listen 80% of the time, and talk 20% of the time.** Very few people take the time to listen to someone's deepest concerns. Be one of the few. Both you and the mourner are likely to learn as a result.
Say, "Call me if you need anything." Vague offers are meant to be declined, and the mourner will pick up on the cue that you implicitly hope that he or she won't contact you.	**Offer specific help** and take the initiative to call a mourner. If you also respect the survivor's privacy, your concrete assistance with the demands of daily living will be appreciated.
Suggest that time heals all wounds. The wounds of loss never completely heal, and grief work is more active than this phrase suggests.	**Expect future 'rough spots'**, with active attempts at coping with difficult feelings and decisions for months following the loss.
Delegate helping to others. Your personal presence and concern will make a difference.	**'Be there' for the mourner.** There are few rules for helping aside from openness and caring.
Say, "I know how you feel." Each griever's experience of grief is unique, so invite the mourner to share his or her feelings, rather than presuming that you know what the issues are for that person.	**Talk about your own losses** and how you have adapted to them. Although the mourner's coping style may be different from your own, your self-disclosure will help.
Use hackneyed consolation, by saying: "There are other fish in the sea," or "God works in mysterious ways." This only convinces the mourner that you do not care enough to understand.	**Use appropriate physical contact**—like an arm around the shoulder or a hug—when words fail. Learn to be comfortable with shared silence, rather than chattering away in an attempt to cheer the person up.

Don't	Do
Try to hurry the person through grief by urging that he or she get busy, give away the deceased's possessions, etc. Grief work takes time and patience and cannot be done on a fixed schedule.	**Be patient with the griever's story**, and allow him or her to share memories of the lost loved one. This fosters a healthy continuity as the person orients to a changed future.

In reading Dr. Neimeyer's words, I remember early after Michael's death, when the topic of saying thank you was very much on my mind and causing me a great deal of concern. So many people supported Michael, Diana and me over the years that I genuinely had no idea how to thank them from a deep place within. How does one truly thank people for this kind of invaluable support?

A good friend who has provided me with a lot of support says, "You should send thank-you cards, especially to Michael's professional bodies." I take this 'should' as a kind of stick to beat myself with. I feel additional pressure fall onto my shoulders: how and when am I going to do this on top of everything else?

During my therapeutic training, we referred to such critical 'should' messages as 'top dog' ones, meaning that we turn criticisms internally in a way that is unhelpful. In this case, my friend's words tap into an internal 'top dog' message that 'I should be getting myself together by now.' I decide to firmly stand my internal ground, to say "no".

Harold's wife, Ruth, sent out a general typed thank-you note immediately after Harold's funeral service. My response on receiving this note had been to feel absolutely amazed that she had managed to 'get her act together' to do this. I am thinking of making the process of saying thank you a gradual and personal one, trusting that people will allow me to lean for a little longer on their support.

It is one and a half years after Michael's death when I actually write my thank-you messages to those professional bodies who gave me some financial support. One of these publishes my note in their professional journal. In it I am able to offer valuable information to readers on realistic expectations regarding the time needed for grieving and a gift of a book that I am working on with The University of Hong Kong. I would not have been in a position to provide this support if I had sent an immediate 'thank you'.

Thus I am reminded that there is absolutely no 'right' and 'wrong': the timing of an action simply is what it is and I have not lost any good friends (my worst fear—the fear of loss) in taking my own time to respond in my own way. I realise that people have all kinds of social expectations and that it is important for me to learn when and how to switch off from these demands of others, even when they are good friends, so that I can care for myself and for my own sense of pace.

SIX MONTHS AFTER MICHAEL'S DEATH

To mark the six-month anniversary of Michael's death, Alicia asks Diana to write a letter to her dad and suggests that she might send it to him with balloons. The letter is heavy in weight so we need to buy more helium balloons. After attaching about eight balloons, Diana lets it go from our roof. It is so wonderful to watch the letter and the balloons fly away after nearly getting stuck on the trees. Finally it drifts right out over and across the mountain. Diana keeps the information in the letter private. It is her personal letter to her dad.

A few weeks later Diana and I go to our favourite noodle shop in Tsing Yi. We are both quite shocked to learn that the nearby Toys 'R' Us shop has closed down. We have spent a lot of time in there whilst she has been growing up, and both feel quite sad as we share memories of shopping there. As we talk, Diana reminds me that the helium balloons were the very last items that we bought from this shop. This is another poignant moment of ending and change in our lives.

Michael's Birth Date
22nd March 2008

It was way past midnight
And she still couldn't fall asleep.

This night the dream was leaving
She tried so hard to keep.

Double
'The Captain of Her Heart'

It's 22nd March 2008, the day that would have been Michael's 47th birthday. I'm trickling the sand through my toes as I sit at the empty end of the beach looking out to sea; my friend's brother is sitting a respectful distance behind me, watching over me as I gaze out over the setting sun in a provincial resort, San Miguel (Saint Michael) in the Philippines.

It seems surreal to me that I am here on this day of all days— somewhere in the world where I have never been before and where so much serves as a reminder of Michael. Not only is there a memorial to Saint Michael as you enter the village but also, on the way to the beach, a jeepney, one of the shiny silver local vehicles, passes by me with 'Michael' written in large letters across the front.

* * *

How did I end up here? On a Tuesday morning a few weeks before in Hong Kong, I drove Diana, Susanne and Noel to school, spent some time chatting with the teachers and then headed for a relaxing coffee in my favourite coffee spot in Mui Wo—Café Paradiso, run by a lovely man called Tom.

I have been deliberately creating 'spaces' in my life, spaces where I step away from the mountain of different burdens and responsibilities. Making time for coffee might seem like an everyday occurrence to most readers. In my case, I have been living moment to moment in a state of trauma for so very long that it really is not easy to create such 'spaces'. Ironically, I feel increased anxiety at such times—my fight-or-flight hormones are so well-trained that I don't trust that it is okay to relax. Too many times when we have started to relax, Michael's cancer returned. The work for me is in learning how to relax again in my life—how to create more of a sense of the normality that most other people live with.

It is during one of these 'spaces' on a Tuesday morning over coffee that I bump unexpectedly into our friend and lawyer, Stephen. Stephen and JoJi's daughter, Sabrina, is one of Diana's closest friends. Diana is totally at home in their family, as am I. As he is describing their new home in Manila, with its restful environment and private swimming pool, he reminds me that we are welcome to visit any time. It dawns on me that we have no plans for Easter. A few e-mails, phone calls and an online flight booking later, Diana and I are on our way to Manila.

Grace's husband, Jun, lends me supportive words: "Don't plan. Do." I recognise that I do currently have a broad plan in my life, which is to connect as much as possible with close friends and family around the world, so that Diana and I feel part of, and held by, a bigger family beyond her and me. I also want Diana to know for sure how she is loved by others in the event of anything happening to me, God forgive. Yet, I haven't had the energy to achieve this plan.

* * *

Once again, by being open to new experiences, the subsequent natural flow of events, and meaningful coincidence, here we are remembering Michael in Diana's friend's home village in San Miguel on the other side of the world from where he and I were born and raised.

As the gentle waves ebb and flow onto the beach, I remember the crystal that I threw into the sea in memory of Michael at his ceremony in Tong Fuk back in October 2007, I remember my friend Lucinda paying her respects by the sea in New Zealand, and I recall the moment of Michael's dying.

As I watch the natural movement of the ocean, the words and music of a song flow into my mind:

> As the day came up she made a start.
> She stopped waiting another day for the captain of her heart.

It is a song by Double called 'The Captain of Her Heart' that was playing many years ago when I fell in love in my 20s in Paris. The memory of another love lost comes to me now—beginnings and endings, all part of the natural flow of life. It was my last significant relationship before Michael, and I remember how much I had wanted the natural flow of life to stop when the relationship had ended.

My view is different now. In this moment, I can look at that memory and my current feelings from a place of greater acceptance. Time simply is what it is—no more, no less. Each moment comes and goes, ebbs and flows like the waves of the sea. We can seek to influence its direction yet ultimately the power and pull of nature is strong.

I completely relax during this time with our friends in the Philippines. Immediately after returning home, however, I am knocked straight off balance again, unable to sleep, tossing and turning at night. I awake to a deep dream.

In the dream, I am in a caravan and camping park. I am talking with Jim, Diana's teacher. He asks how I am and I tell him what a great time I am having.

He is taken aback and asks, "What about the earthquake?"

"What earthquake?" I reply.

He points to the ground and, as we walk, shows me where a massive earthquake has cracked open large holes in the ground in between the caravans.

I see inside my caravan where my friends are drinking, laughing and having fun. I feel immediately shocked, judging this behaviour as deeply inappropriate. How can they be so disconnected from what is happening? How can we not have seen this? I watch as an electricity pylon is about to crash down on top of my caravan. I rush to help everyone to escape. Real danger is all around and yet we hadn't even noticed it.

I talk about my dream with Ceci. I recognise how I feel guilty having fun when there is something as major as an earthquake happening around me and I'm not even aware of it. I am creating time for relaxation and fun in my life yet, deep inside of me, permission is not given for this. This is the first dream that I have shared with Ceci, although dream work has been a part of my psychotherapy training and practice for many years and is an aspect of my work that I love.

Ceci reminds me how all the elements in the dream represent parts of me and how important it is to recognise and to acknowledge these. She asks me to imagine myself as the earthquake. In so doing, I connect with my power, strong emotions, a tremendous force of change that is determined to find expression at whatever cost—a force of nature too strong to ignore.

The dream represents different aspects of my experience. We look at the character of Sandra's response to the power of her emotional change in the dream. 'Sandra' has not even seen her power and force; she is blind to it and then feels shocked, guilty and frightened that she has not noticed that she is seeking escape from these feelings.

Ceci then guides me to forge a different relationship with my powerful feelings and emotions, to acknowledge them and to support myself in receiving them.

TAKING TIME OUT

I recognise what an incredible ten-year journey Diana and I have been on and, metaphorically and emotionally, want to stop and get off the world for a while. In my twenties, when I faced a time of significant change, I simply packed a rucksack and went travelling. I now hold too many responsibilities to do this. Instead, I determine that, for the first time since we arrive in Hong Kong, I'll take a full two months off work in the summer.

We spend two wonderful weeks with my cousin Trevor, his wife Lynne and their two boys, Thomas and Michael, at the start of July when they visit us for the first time in Hong Kong. I then plan a wonderful trip around Europe staying with my closest friends and visiting family. We spend a long time with Valerie and her family in their holiday home in France, and I take Diana to one of my favourite cities in the world, Paris, where we also meet up with Kate and her children. We savour every moment of the summer and whilst I wish that it could go on forever, it really does help to start to feed and nourish me—at long last.

Writing about our summer reminds me that a wise friend told me, "Don't make any major decisions at this early stage in your grieving." I am so grateful for this. One of the major decisions that I am facing is whether to stay in Hong Kong—where home no longer feels like home—or to move back to Europe. My emotions ebb and flow dramatically on this subject and, with my friend's advice, I make a firm decision *not* to make any major decisions in my life for the next two years. While staying in Hong Kong, I have also retained close connections with my friends in the UK and Europe since Michael died, and I now make more frequent trips to London where I love to meet my good friends such as Karen, Valerie, Julie and Steve in Clapham. I recognise that it's important for me to keep a foot in both cities: London and Hong Kong.

FEELING EMOTIONALLY RAW

The only part of the summer trip that I don't savour is the time spent clearing the garage of our home in the UK, the first home that Michael and I lived in together. I feel a sense of impending dread about this and it is much worse than I imagined. I stay with good friends Jane and Mike. Jane looks after Diana whilst Mike and I empty the garage. I arrive at the house alone. As I walk towards our back garden gate, it is as if time has stood still and Michael is about to walk out into the garden to meet and kiss me.

The emotional intensity of this moment bowls me over; my sense of reality is changed in a split second. I stand still, lost, not knowing how to handle this experience.

A few minutes later, our former neighbour walks out of his drive and says hello to me. Still I feel as if I am in a surreal, parallel universe. I have not seen this neighbour since Michael and I left for Hong Kong.

Then, as at other deeply intense emotional moments in my life, a wonderful and unexpected synchronicity occurs. My neighbour shows me one of his cats on the wall and reminds me that this is one of the kittens we gave to him when we left. He tells me that the mother cat, which we also gave to him, lost her leg in an accident so she is now a three-legged cat. Again I face another moment of poignant synchronicity—both Michael and our cat lost a leg. As soon as I see the now three-legged cat, I am aware how much she looks like a sister to Flakes, the first abandoned cat that we gave a home to in Hong Kong.

Thank goodness Mike turns up to help me to clear the garage! He has brought a flask of coffee and all sorts of practical gadgets and tools to help us to get through the job. We are even able to laugh a lot along the way about the things that we find.

Later that day when I hope to relax, Jane receives a telephone call and immediately breaks down in tears. One of her son's closest friends is on holiday with his father in Egypt. The local bus in which they are travelling has crashed and his friend has been killed instantly.

What! Immediately, friends on whom I was hoping to lean for support are themselves experiencing trauma and grief. It feels like too much to bear. As I hand some of our possessions to local charities and send others back to Hong Kong, I feel as if my feet are lead weights and I can barely move forwards. To cap it all, Diana gets a tooth abscess and we have to book her into the dentist for a very painful extraction.

As Time Passes By
2008

There is pleasure in the pathless woods
There is rapture on the lonely shore
There is society, where none intrudes
By the deep sea, and music in its roar
I love not man the less but Nature more.

Lord Byron
'There is Pleasure in the Pathless Woods'

As time passes by, I begin to gradually turn more outwards than inwards. Time spent alone and resting continues to be important, although time spent with good friends steadily becomes equally—and then even more—important to me. Diana has settled well into school; I am back at work. I continue to have significant pressures on my time due to all the continued legal, financial and administrative pressures that I still hate. One of my greatest concerns at this time is how to best pace all the different pressures that I face, although there are rare glimpses of balance from time to time.

I have been sharing my experiences of bereavement with the University of Hong Kong over the past two years to help in the creation of teaching films and materials to assist others in a similar situation to me. Looking back at the films I am struck by just how exhausted and run-down I look, how my hair needs cutting, how I haven't spent much time on make-up. I have gradually changed since the making of these films, investing in caring for myself, and in wanting to look good again. I refer to these kinds of activities as 'feeding myself'. These words are a good metaphor, as I also gradually find myself regaining my appetite.

Friends ask if it helps me to imagine Michael being with me and to imagine speaking with him and asking for his support. Michael's

Aunt Jeanette is very clear that she often speaks with her husband who passed away many years before. I smile when she tells me how she carries so many pressures that some days she just imagines saying to him, "See, if you were here then I wouldn't have to do this!"

Although she and others find comfort in imagining their husband's presence, this is not the case for me. I know that Michael is gone and the truth of that fact feels very painful to me. Imagining that he is not gone feels crazy-making. It is hard enough to be letting go without starting to imagine that he hasn't gone. I don't know if my relationship with Michael's absence will change over time. I suppose that it might.

* * *

In a recent workshop held by Dr. Robert Neimeyer that I attended in Hong Kong, I worked on my memories and my experience of my Uncle Bill's death when I was in my twenties.

It was particularly shocking for me. He awoke in the night thinking he had indigestion and took a tablet. He was actually having a heart attack and died. I was living with three close girlfriends in a shared house at the University of Edinburgh when the call came through from my parents in the early hours of the morning—another moment in my life that I'll never forget.

For the first time in over twenty years since his death, my memories of my Uncle Bill's supportive presence in my life come back to me. I feel him here with me now, just as he was there for me when I was a child.

* * *

I am feeling really good in the run-up to the anniversary of Michael's death. I can see the progress that I have made in my life. I feel proud of myself. Then, out of the blue, sometime towards the end of August 2008, the stark emotional reality of my loss hits me again as if from nowhere. I feel really angry with the universe, with life, with everyone—and I cannot stop crying. I really thought that I had my emotions under control. I don't at all.

I seek to manage this first anniversary by setting plans in place for how to spend the day on 6th September 2008. My new friend Justina is holding a mass in a Catholic cathedral in memory of her husband TP. She offers to dedicate the mass to Michael as well as to TP, and invites me to join her and her family for the morning. I find this a wonderful and incredibly kind and supportive gesture.

I ask Diana how she wants to spend the day: she wants to go ice-skating with Susanne. I also discuss with Paddy and Barbara how we might spend the day. I have been talking about where to keep all the special things that we have to remember Michael, and they have a lovely suggestion that we make a trip to the antique shop in Mui Wo to buy a chest to keep these items in.

As I think about the day I also realise how I would really like another friend to be with me for the Hong Kong part of the day: the mass and also the ice rink. I have a particular friend in mind and ask if she will join me. My request is short notice. She doesn't feel comfortable about attending the mass, but agrees to join me for coffee later on, despite already having an important business meeting in place. My friend, also grieving Michael's loss, has the emotional response of feeling 'hemmed in'. She does not feel comfortable saying 'no', as this is Michael's anniversary and she fears a strong emotional response from me, and is finding my expectations to be too high. I have not thought or planned ahead. I am responding to my needs only as these emerge and I am not seeing clearly.

On the morning of 6th September 2008, Diana, Susanne and I attend the morning mass for TP and Michael. The moment that I set foot inside the cathedral and see Justina, I begin to sob. I can barely speak to her. Justina cries too. The mass is so warm and comforting. I feel relieved that Diana has Susanne by her side for company.

* * *

I am reminded in writing these words how Jim, Diana's teacher, told me how they were discussing smoking and health one day in class, not long after Michael died. Diana had her hand up all the time wanting to speak. When Jim invited her to do so she began to talk about her dad and his cancer.

Jim said, "The whole class fell immediately and uncommonly silent, listening intently to Diana, knowing how her dad had recently died."

The care, concern and respect of the other children for Diana were so evident and strong.

* * *

Diana and Susanne start to feel bored during the mass and ask if they can go outside to play. I say yes, feeling my own relief to have more personal space. I sit quietly as Justina's family and friends pay their respects to her as they leave the service.

I then walk up to Justina. We hug each other, with the tears continuing to flow. Without need for words, or explanation, or apology, only the deepest form of shared empathy and understanding, we hold each other tightly and we cry. I mean that we really, really cry, loud and hard, without embarrassment, taking all the time that we want to do so. It is an incredibly precious moment for me. Once again, by meaningful coincidence, we have come into each other's lives and are able to offer something in this moment that others cannot understand in exactly the same way. Together we find mutual comfort in the company of Justina's family and friends.

Once outside the cathedral, with the children feeling excited and impatient to go ice-skating, I call my friend to check on our coffee plans. She explains that something else has come up and gives me her apologies.

In the normal run of events, this is a natural occurrence, yet not today, not for me. I immediately feel hurt and angry. My friend is also angry. She tells me that I am expecting too much from her and that we didn't make a firm commitment. I help the girls on with their ice skates and sit in the coffee bar by the side of the rink—alone. I watch the girls laughing, smiling and having so much fun together as they skate past me. The contrast with my feelings of loneliness is so acutely painful, especially after just leaving the warm embrace of the cathedral. In the absence of friends physically sitting with me, I phone them and they help me to calm down.

* * *

It is only days and weeks later that I feel calmer, more ready to learn from this experience and I am still learning now. It is absolutely true that, at this time, I have very little space to listen to others' feelings. My friend was also a good friend of Michael's. She is grieving too. Yet I am selfish. It takes me all that I have to support and listen to Diana and me. I want others to take care of themselves and, if anything, to put us first and help us because we hurt the most. Given the strength and depth of my emotions at this time, there is little that I can take in.

Looking back now I still do not recall the specific details of what happened in the way that my friend can. This incident also raises important issues relating to different senses of timing and expectations that clash readily when tensions are high. I wanted my friend to be there for me at this time; she felt pressure from my expectations, finding them to be unrealistic. I see how, at such times, issues take on disproportionate dimensions.

* * *

After the ice-skating and lunch with the children, I feel completely drained emotionally and all I want to do is go home and rest. Barbara and Paddy suggest that we leave shopping for the chest until the next day; this is a wonderful suggestion.

The next morning, we have a lovely, relaxing breakfast and head off to the small antiques shop. Paddy and Barbara know the owners well. I already have in mind some ideas about Tibetan chests, but Diana does not like these as she finds some of the images on them too frightening. I see what she means. She searches in a corner and then shows me the chest that she would like. It is a Chinese camphor chest and it is absolutely perfect: the camphor will help to protect the items inside and the chest will fit well in our living room.

Once home, we put it in the middle of the living room, where we plan to use it as a coffee table. Memories of Michael will thus remain in the centre of our home. Diana immediately lounges on the sofa and puts her feet up on the chest. It feels just right—a perfect choice!

My Journey and Change
2009

Do not follow where the path may lead. Go instead where there is no path and leave a trail.

Muriel Strode

As I write this section of my book, it is twenty-one months since Michael died. Diana and I face another 'ending' as she graduates from primary school.

I remain sensitive to 'endings' and one of the main physical effects is tension manifested in my shoulders and neck. I see this as a response to my having 'shouldered' so much over the past years, so I look after myself by attending a good physiotherapy practice here in Hong Kong. As the therapist helps me to relieve the tension in my muscles, there is also a release of the emotional pain that has led to the tension in the first place.

This emotional release is evident in my dream:

I am with my friend Karen, my friend who has been by my side for many important and emotional experiences in my life. We are on the beach and look up to see a gigantic wave looming up above our heads, still in the distance, yet moving towards us. We realise that we are in a tsunami. We look at each other and know that we need to make a choice on where to run: away from or into the darkness of the wave. We choose to run into the wave.

The dream is long, and throughout the whole dream we know that we are still under the wave. At times, parts of the wave crash down on us like a waterfall. At times, we find temporary places to rest. At others, we are sent over the edge, free-floating into oblivion, and at one stage we catch onto rubber tyres as we fall and they slow down the pace of our fall.

Throughout the dream, there are times when I realise that I am separated from Diana, that I don't know where she is. At these times, I start to feel complete and utter despair to a depth that I find impossible to bear. It is Karen who encourages me to go on.

She says, "We have come this far. Don't give up now. You have to trust and believe that we will find Diana." I realise that giving up will not help me and I find renewed energy.

Towards the end of the dream, we are no longer sure even what part of the world we are in as we have travelled so far. We see a family eating food and then realise how starving we are. We have no memory of when we last ate yet have not noticed this until now. We ask if we might share food with the family. They welcome us, asking if we can also help them later to find canvas to protect us all from the broken glass that they anticipate coming our way shortly.

We learn that we are in Essex, in the UK, and how the family has had some time to prepare for this tidal wave that is sweeping across the world, as it started in Hong Kong. The power and height of the wave are lower now, yet Karen and I know throughout the dream that we are still under it. We have only had fleeting glimpses of the sky that have quickly dissipated as we crash back under the wave. What we learn now is that the power of the wave is lessening so that we have some momentary breathing space, food and rest. I realise how very tired I am and wonder if there will be time to sleep a while before we search for the canvas.

I wake from the dream with the sensation of still living under the wave.

I share my dream with Charles who directs to me the front page of his website[1]. Here he uses Hokusai's famous image of the *Great Wave off Kanagawa* to represent the continuing process of growth and change in our lives. He points out the boats in the tsunami, with people clinging together and insisting on surviving it all.

I am reminded that I am still grieving while I have also travelled a long way and am still travelling. I have grown and changed over this time. I feel happier and more confident. I have much more energy. I am finding meaning and fulfilment in my role as a mother and in

[1]   http://www.charles-neal.com

writing my book. I have found fresh motivation and challenge in my human resources work. I am happy again in my home and am building a new life. I have more financial stability. I'm spending much more time with my friends and on social activities, and I'm really relaxing and enjoying this. I feel my life becoming more 'normal', albeit that I continue to live under 'waves' that also still crash over and into me from time to time. Our lives now have more happy events in them and new beginnings as well as new endings. I am also delighted to share that our friend Colin is living cancer-free at this date and that Jodi-Ann's cancer is in remission.

My journey of change over these past two years is wonderfully illustrated in a story that an Australian friend told me recently one night in The Gallery. He is a new friend whom I have only come to know over the two years since Michael died.

> I remember when you first used to come into The Gallery and be happier to sit alone reading your book. We would talk to you from the bar and you would talk back yet you wouldn't come and sit with us. As time passed, you would edge closer and closer towards us, moving from table four to table three to table two, to table one.... Then finally, one day, you decided to sit up at the bar and join us. Now you are happy to walk in here and to take your place at the bar.

I respond to his story, explaining how, as a woman, I still don't necessarily feel very comfortable sitting at the bar on my own. I feel concerned: "What will people think of me?"

He replies, "They will think that you are a local and you are."

I really appreciate his encouraging words as well as the amusing way that he tells this story. I feel grateful to him for his support. I do now feel at home in my local bar, indeed sometimes too at home!

As for Diana's ongoing journey, she is growing into a pretty and confident pre-teen. She is increasingly independent, enjoying her life and her friends. I feel so very proud of her and love her very much.

Diana's grief also continues to manifest in different ways. She recently asked me if she could take her dad's perfume from my room to spray onto her pillow so that she can remember him.

I say, "Daddy would call it aftershave rather than perfume, and yes, of course you can take it."

Later that night when I wander into her room to kiss her goodnight, she is curled up on her pillow, which smells strongly of one of Michael's aftershaves that I love. She is cuddling the soft blue bear that she gave to Michael when he died.

I feel as if my own heart is breaking inside. I would give anything in the world to be able to bring her daddy back to her. I also know that I never can and I feel so very proud of her creativity in finding ways to support herself. I see how we are each learning to find our new independent paths in the world.

Moving On
2010 Onwards

Change your heart, look around you.
Change your heart, it will astound you.

The Korgis
'Everybody's Got to Learn Sometime'

In accepting and embracing the waves of emotional change, I discover that there are new feelings that have been gradually emerging and taking the place of grief. These include feelings of passion, desire and sensuality. It is both wonderful and indeed anxiety-provoking to feel these again. I am reminded of me as a woman in my twenties. I feel a renewed spirit of youthfulness, bringing with it a sense of long-forgotten excitement, together with anxieties similar to those that I had as a teenager. And I thought that my teenage years were long past!

The words of a song come into my mind:

You've done too much much too young.
You're married with a kid
When you should be having fun with me.

The Specials
'Too Much Too Young'

The emergence of these lyrics surprises me like my new feelings do. I love Diana very deeply. My relationship with her brings vital meaning in my life. I also loved being married to Michael. Yet there are other emotions inside of me that the spirit of this song captures, including the desire to relax, to enjoy life, to have some fun and indeed to fall in love again. I am still young.

So where do I go from here? I have no more of a compass for navigating the emergence and expression of these new emotions and this next stage in my life than I have had any kind of map for my life so far. I have even less experience of being single and knowing how to date. It is little wonder that I am reminded of being in my twenties, as it was then that I was single.

What I do know for sure, however, is that there are worse experiences that life can throw in my direction than learning how to handle renewed feelings of passion. And goodness only knows that I've learned how to handle pain!

At this moment in time I do not face daily medical traumas. I have a successful career, doing work that I enjoy with colleagues whom I respect and care for. I have a lovely home and good friends living in different countries in the world. I have a wonderful, fit and healthy daughter. I'm also fit and healthy myself. Perhaps this might be a time in my life when I can start to relax and enjoy more. I like to hope so.

I notice the words on my calendar:

> Taking chances, both personally and professionally, can be risky, but it's ultimately more rewarding than not even getting into the game.

If I am going to start taking chances then I am very grateful that I have good friends by my side when I do so, and it is with the words of my good friend Rachel that I want to close my book. I called her in one of my "Oh good grief, what am I doing, I'm not ready for this!" moments.

Her reply: "You know what, Sandra? At least you know that you are *living*."

Appendix I
GET SET & GO in Bereavement
By Professor Cecilia Lai Wan Chan

Appendix II
Resources for Bereavement Support

GET SET & GO in Bereavement

By Professor Cecilia Lai Wan Chan

The Get SET & Go programme seeks to facilitate individuals in **S**urviving, **E**mpowering and **T**ransforming **Go**als through the process of end-of-life care, the death of their spouse, as well as their own bereavement process.

There are many beautiful stories about smooth and transforming bereavement experiences. There may be tearful moments and also sweet memories of having spent a lifetime with the deceased.

In Sandra's case, she organised a memorial on the beach in the community where she lived. 150 friends attended this very beautiful occasion. The following is taken verbatim from an interview with Sandra six months after Michael Keys died.

1. BE PREPARED FOR CHAOS

No matter how prepared one may be, the moment of death and the loss of a loved one can be disabling. Multiple tasks and decisions to make regarding the funeral, estate management, practical arrangements in everyday life when bank accounts are frozen, what to do on the weekends, loss of adult-to-adult communication at home, no one to ask advice from or quarrel with, empty bed and chairs, disruption of daily routines, sleepless nights... Gather social support and seek help, as there are many decisions and practical arrangements to be made.

[On sorting out possessions]

Sandra: It's a lot and everything else is still waiting to be done. And that's six months and we've got half a bag to go and a pile of things that I'm wearing. And I've got one wardrobe of his which I have now emptied of the stuff we're clearing, so I can begin to put new things in that I've been buying for me, which gives me a feeling of bringing in newness as well as clearing old things.

But that, I mean, that's very slow, and yet that's, we seem to be, well we're not, we're not clearing things fast, but we've got a pace... It bothers me a bit more, I think. Yeah, I clearly want to, somehow or other, want to be clearing things fast. Which I think is an expression of my discomfort with the feelings, and not wanting them, because actually in truth when I start to do the things it's very emotionally draining...

[On managing money]

Sandra: My husband is good, was good, with money, so he'd actually handle a lot of that. We'd talk about it, but more of that would be on his shoulders than mine. So suddenly having all the accountability for financial decision-making is quite new to me.

I asked her [a friend], she'd already offered to be by my side, someone I could talk to in the way I used to with Michael. And I asked her specifically could I share my financial and legal issues with her. So she helped hold them with me, and she's been more than happy to do that. But for a lot of the time that's no more than putting it in an e-mail, making a phone call every now and again, but I have a feeling that I am not alone.

And the other thing around that is I've got a lot of effort in managing, and now we've got a good bookkeeper in place which we didn't have. There's the end-of-year audit for business and I've now invited another accountant to kind of act as an advisor. So I'll meet with him quarterly so he can look at the business monies with me.

2. AT EASE WITH EMOTIONAL SWINGS

Tears can stream down upon memory of the deceased. There may be peaceful moments, and yet, the sharp pain of sadness and strong sense of loss can also be overwhelming. The difficulty is to appreciate such a tsunami of unfamiliar emotions. Individuals can feel at a complete loss and be confused. Some may be totally disillusioned and lose confidence in their ability to solve problems and make decisions.

Sandra: ...the extremity of the swing is very fast from one day to the other. That's bad... Yeah, its more, there's a lot of emotional pendulum, kind of swing, and not so much kind of steady, this is the way things are. Everything is up in the air, everything…

Very vulnerable, because that's when one emotional thing hits, it's suddenly connecting again with those deep feelings that go when I was by the side of Michael dying, knowing the reality of death because that for me dying is an experience that I haven't gone through personally but that I've shared intimately with someone else so I certainly know it and experience it to be real.

It's not a fantasy or something I am in denial of. But these emotional things can then immediately trigger those deep existential feelings, of we come into this life alone, we go out of it alone. Yeah, I can be right in that place and then remind myself, "Okay, I am alive and I am not alone," and actually, these connections are very important. But certain things can trigger—yeah, I don't even know how to describe it—this darkness of that experience, that reality, that truth. Not good or bad, [but] a very particular emotional place, reality.

3. REALISTIC STRESS INOCULATION

It will be helpful to provide family members with psychological preparation on tasks and emotional responses during bereavement. Physical exhaustion is common because of the unsolicited volunteered advice from friends and family members. Naming their mixed emotions can help the bereaved be at greater ease with emotions feeling out of control.

[About thinking of whether to migrate back to the UK or stay in Hong Kong]

Sandra: Your sharing on the physical and emotional exhaustion after the memorial, the loneliness, the packing of materials of Michael were actually helpful… It's actually a time for me to come down, to allow myself to rest, to heal, therefore moving house, moving home, moving job, all those other big stresses don't actually feature in that.

So I guess I've supported myself by labelling, you know, for two years, two to three years I won't make any big decisions, which fits with Diana finishing primary school, so that's, you know, a natural transition in our life anyway. […] I like that decision, I think that's a good decision. It also brings with it a certain amount of emotional rollercoaster…

Yes, it's in those moments, it's like all those abandonment feelings that go back years, as being adopted as a baby, kind of feeling like everything goes from under me. Which you know, it's not true… change brings what it brings, just don't know what it is.

Cecilia: You are a talented woman, with inner and outer beauty…. You are always warm…. You have enormous caring for other people. You always want to be of help. You worked really hard in order to help yourself…

Sandra: That's true.

Cecilia: And you have learned to pace yourself and accept yourself unconditionally. Bereavement is a totally new experience for which you have not gone through any training at all. It's so insecure, it hurts so much. And it's these complex emotions of fear, anxiety, uncomfortableness, irritation, everything, bitterness.

Sandra: Yeap, anger…

Cecilia: Jealousy…. It's such a combo of negative emotions that is overwhelming.

Sandra: Yeap. Therefore trust and appreciate yourself that you have actually gone through it with a lot of grace.

Sandra: Thanks, I can see that I am doing that, you know. Which was one of the things I actually put in on the list here. Because a part of doing that has been to… 'cause I still have all those responsibilities to hold. In the past, my default would be just to work hard, push through, and I have had absolutely no willpower to push myself anywhere, so that message doesn't even get through my brain. The message that is getting through instead is: "No way, no way. You look after yourself."

4. SURVIVING INTENSE FEAR

The bereavement experience shatters the sense of safety, predictability, control and security. Bereaved persons can easily be paralysed by panic. Worry about one's own health, the present and the future can be disabling. In response to fear, they can become anxious and engage themselves into endless searching for remedies to reduce fear. This bias for action may not be most helpful. Recognising the sense of fear and the loss of sense of control are the first steps to coping with fear of further losses. Befriending fear and listening to its voice can help the bereaved feel more comfortable with themselves and their emotions.

Sandra: Fear is my biggest enemy. Yes, that's the one I am most consistently working on, am aware of, am conscious of when it happens. Yet somatically when times are stressed my body will have moved into that [fear] by default and I have noticed and pull myself out. Fear is definitely, you know, if I was more connected, I think of fear and excitement on a pendulum. If I was more attuned to the excitement end... but fear is my enemy.

Cecilia: And how do you help yourself to stay with the fear, if you don't take it as an enemy? If you take 'fear of abandonment' as a friend?

Sandra: What I usually say around fear, is kind of feel the fear, sort of feel the fear, acknowledge it and make decisions and do what I want to do still so don't let the fear disable me but just recognise it's there. Thinking of 'fear of abandonment' as a friend. Well what that does for me or part of what it does for me is that I invest time on connections and contacts because they are what nourish me and keep me alive, and make life what it is that's valuable.

Cecilia: So it actually helps you recognise your need to be connected.

Sandra: To be connected, yes, and the criticalness of that actually that's what life is about is that connection.

Cecilia: And wanting to gives you the energy to...

Sandra: To act, yeah, to do, feel the fear, do it anyway. Reach out, get what I need, it motivates me to act. That's always been the response actually. I see the pros, but that can actually lead to the over-productive, fast-moving, which I'm really proactively.... Yeah, I don't freeze with fear I just get very fast, busy. But I'm really challenging that.

Cecilia: So if I, if I ask you to say something to your fear in terms of very grateful to your fear, what would you be grateful [for]?

Sandra: Actually that's very interesting. I'm very grateful that you've kept me alive.... I'm very grateful that you've kept me alive. Interesting. I'm very grateful that you've sustained and energised me. Grateful that you challenge me. That's interesting. None of that is frightening at all actually. You challenge me, motivate me, lead me to new directions, new things, new adventures, lead me to live my life. Grateful that you've helped me to find my way, follow my path, follow my heart. That's amazing. Gosh. I haven't really thought about fear as a friend. That's interesting. That's quite a concept shift: fear becomes a friend.

Cecilia: It has given you energy that you won't have otherwise to move you out of the comfort zones.

Sandra: Definitely and to overcome incredible events in life, life and death events, and to find strengths I didn't know I had in me…. 'Cause the fear is real, it's appropriate, until it becomes more intense than is appropriate for the situation but it's still a real feeling. No, that's cool.

Thanks Ceci, that's quite amazing actually. I am going to stay with that concept shift. What made you think of that, to see fear as a friend? To be accepting of the feeling rather than to treat it as an enemy? 'Cause I am more often treating it as an enemy, attacking it. Criticising it. Instead of valuing the information that it's giving me. If I listen to the information that it's giving me, it's going to take care of me. If Diana feels frightened, I take care of her. I look at what's frightening her and check out the situation. See what she needs. Okay, that's pretty cool.

5. SURVIVING INTENSE ANGER

"Why?" "Why me?" During loss of a loved one, especially when the loss is unexpected and sudden, a bereaved person can become very angry, highly irritable, aggressive, verbally abusive, fault-finding and intolerant of mistakes. It is easy for some, among those who are furiously angry, to find the whole world being unjust. There is also a strong negative impulse to destroy and ruin.

Anger can also fuel constructive actions for change. Learning assertiveness techniques can help people communicate anger in a positive and constructive way in relationships, and to realise that anger is healthy, yet aggression is not. Anger and frustrations can also be expressed in the form of physical activities, such as sports, dance and volunteerism. Their anger can be turned into righteous action to restore justice and benevolent acts of charity to help people in the same boat. Some bereaved persons are fatalistically angry at God or the heavens or at the deceased persons who abandoned the family. Meaning-searching, activities such as journaling, can help bereaved persons in dealing with such angry emotions. Meditation, yoga and mindfulness activities also help.

Sandra saw a friend at the airport when she returned from Michael's funeral in the UK. The friend asked, "How's it going?" in a casual manner. Sandra did not know how to respond and was frozen. She was in deep grief right after Michael's burial and her life was miserable. This ordinary 'hello and goodbye' greeting hurt tremendously and Sandra was angry that this friend was insensitive to her state of emotions.

Through our discussion, we agreed that since bereavement is such a topic that is so rarely discussed in public, people simply do not know what to say to bereaved persons: what helps and what hurts. Sandra agreed to keep a journal of her bereavement experience and share it with other people so that the general population can be more sensitive to the needs of bereaved persons.

6. COPING WITH SWEET MEMORIES TWINNED WITH THE EXPERIENCE OF GRIEF

A continuing bond with the deceased is also a bittersweet experience. Familiar places, objects, thoughts that remind bereaved persons of the deceased are hard to endure. Initial intrusive thoughts of the deceased hurt a lot as every thought reminds them of their loss. By attempting to raise the profile of the positive and appreciative thoughts of the living legacy of the deceased, bereaved persons can slowly enhance the sweetness to the bitter loss.

> [About missing a friend who came to visit six months after Michael's death and then returned to Europe]
>
> **Sandra:** You know, that's also kind of bittersweet. It's nice [to have visitors] and then it's upsetting [to see them go], and it's not stable, it's not.
>
> **Cecilia:** It's harder to say goodbye. It's good to have comforting relationships, but [when] it comes to say goodbye it hurts more.
>
> **Sandra:** It hurts more. It's really like a mini bereavement. Actually, that would make sense of the strength of the feelings that came with it.

Cecilia: Because with the bereavement experience, this goodbye is like opening up your old bereavement wounds again. Pain of separation from loved ones, temporary or permanent, is still a separation pain.

Sandra: That makes sense of it actually, because although it's not the same intensity it has those same reminders of the bittersweetness of losing Michael. Yeah. No, that's obviously what's happening. I can see that in different ways actually...

7. ACCEPT VULNERABILITY AND HELP

Bereaved persons can be accident-prone as the loss may cause a short-term physio-immunological suppression, as well as cognitive, psycho-emotional, social and spiritual malfunction. Nurture oneself like a sick person and allow oneself to go through a long rehabilitation process. Keep to a simple daily routine with regular meals and outdoor physical exercise. Accept help from family members and friends, as other people want to be able to help too. There will also be tasks of handling finances and practical housekeeping that bereaved persons are not familiar with, which can be scary.

Sandra: On the legal side of things, very thankfully a good friend helped to do a will before Michael died and became my lawyer. [...] I really trust him and he offers really sound advice, and I've now got his team and me, so although the process is slow I feel held in that process. [...] I invested in paying for his company's corporate team to take off all the corporate affairs stuff off my shoulders so I don't have to carry those.[...] It's not a huge amount of money for the relief it gives me, so all my decisions around that have been about don't do this alone, find trusted people and hand it over and share it.

Cecilia: Seek help.

Sandra: Yeah, seek help, ask for help and everywhere I am doing that, everywhere. I don't feel embarrassed about that because I feel that's kind of helping me keep alive, keep sane, and actually it's making some of these things even slightly enjoyable. You know, funny thing to say, but you know, as I start to look at what I can and can not do with my monies, to share that with someone is more interesting than to sit at home worrying about it, it is just frightening.[...]

Another thing I am going to help myself [with] is making time in the mornings to have space for having a cup of coffee in my favourite coffee shop, and that's led to me spending time with people I don't often see, one of whom is a friend who has a house in the Philippines. And we were maybe going to go there, but it looks like they're probably going away to the States, so now I don't have any plans. But after this recent weekend I'm feeling disappointed that we have no plans. So, I'm now trying to think what to do.

I will come onto the money, which is one of the things on my list here, but this connecting with travelling is a really empowering thing 'cause I have always loved travelling since I was a child. It's just been in my blood and when Michael was really sick we couldn't travel and now that Diana is at this age where, you know she was amazing on this five-hour journey from Manila up to the north of the Philippines. She just, I thought, you know, she actually... takes this in her stride, so she and I can travel.

8. COPE WITH BEREAVEMENT AS IF IT IS A TEMPORARY DISABILITY

As bereaved persons can experience sudden outbursts of emotions, be easily in tears, find it hard to concentrate, get irritated and annoyed easily, as well as feel exhausted, it is essential for them to slow down. They may find themselves becoming antisocial and cynical. There is a strong tendency to hide and avoid meeting people because talking to friends reminds them of their loss. Allow oneself time and space to heal, as the whole family is wounded in the process of witnessing the death of a loved one. Learn to let our loved ones go and allow oneself to move on in life. Like being temporarily disabled after the trauma of bereavement, accept a process of rehabilitation and make room for oneself to grieve and recover.

Sandra: I was thinking back over the six months and social contact has been interesting. In the beginning I didn't want any [social contacts] at all and now I have gradually had a little bit more. Even now I haven't been out in the evening for ages unless it's just locally, because it just doesn't appeal to me at all. But gradually making more time just to hang out, have cups of coffee, chat a bit more to people, that's really nice.

In fact that's now helping me more than hindering me. Just thinking on the social contact. I have been listening to what I want. I haven't been forcing it, which I am quite proud of actually. I haven't said that I have to be out in the evening, or any of that kind of thing. So it seems to be gradually, just gradually taking its own pace. But sometimes I feel stronger in that than others.

One of the things yesterday, which really emotionally knocked me off track is that I've had very good friendships with [xxx] over the years. Talking to them at the start and the end of the day has actually been a huge support for me in different ways. And then this huge thing blew up yesterday, which will blow over and it's only partly me, but lots of people's feelings were upset. I just could not shake it off all day, because I got so frightened that everyone's feelings upset meant I was now going to lose these friends and it was extremely unsettling. [...] So, yeah, the whole upset of that was very unsettling.

So it really affected me, so I had been doing quite, feeling quite disempowered, especially after the holiday and then I was kind of plummeted back into feeling like, whoa, suddenly feeling like nothing is [certain] and I really am at the end of the day now alone.

And in the past if something upsetting had happened like these things do blow up, then always Michael would be there. Always, and always that was one of the strengths in our marriage. We'd talk it through and he would support me and he would help me switch off and move on. And not sit and let it get me down. And, ah, I just missed him so much it was so painful. And because it was people I actually cared about and was leaning on, all the comfort was with... I was just, yeah, like a feeling of my ground going from under me, and knowing, what I kind of know ground is what it is anyway, but just really about existential feeling of ultimate aloneness.

9. ATTEND TO ONE'S OWN NEEDS AND DESIRES

Isolation and loneliness are hard to bear. It is particularly important that physical, psychological, social and spiritual desires are connected. There are cravings for intimacy, for touch and for love.

> **Sandra:** It's a human being thing, but that has been one of the things over the six months that has caused me... you know, a lot of emotional turmoil and still is. I also feel so naïve in this.

I mean I was in my late 20s when I was last single, you know. I don't know what I'm doing even. And if someone says to me now, "Do you want to be dating?" Absolutely no; the very thought of even having dinner in town with friends is enough. So meeting people I don't know, dating, getting rejected, ugh, it's awful.

But the fact [is] that I've developed feelings for someone I care about, who is a friend and those feelings have evolved naturally in me, and represent a craving in me for something that I haven't had for quite a long time and something that I really want.

And then trying to balance both respecting that it's my craving and the reality that this is a friendship and that is, it's both wonderful, it gives me a feeling of being alive, and of knowing that those cravings are real and, you know, as a 44-year-old woman, I do have sexual needs, I do want that in my life, and on the other hand being a bit like a teenager and not knowing where to go with it.

10. PROCESS OF SENSE-MAKING AND MEANING RECONSTRUCTION

In the midst of loss, bereaved persons will try to actively make sense of the situation and to reconstruct meaning in their survival. The process of sense- and meaning-making is not a smooth process. Growth and transformation may move in a spiral process. With good progress, there may be times of regression.

[On her experiences of meaning-making]

Sandra: Interesting, because I wrote down 'channelling my energies into something meaningful'. This is also a pendulum 'cause it's other things like people who talk to me more about cancer now since we were so open. And you know, a good friend of my helper in the village who is now very critically ill and I've been supporting her in different ways. I helped behind the scenes with her fundraising yet I've also kept myself physically distant from her, because it's just so...

Cecilia: So painful.

Sandra: Painful so I've supported from behind the scenes. I did the Cancer Link thing yesterday to the help that you gave me earlier and we talked about it, things like that, you know, and I have to just watch that because I want to be able to support people but I equally will find myself getting very overwhelmed and very tired.

11. IGNORE UNSOLICITED ADVICE ON HOW TO GRIEVE

People may volunteer advice on how and when to grieve, as well as when to stop grieving. Such comments and suggestions often lead to feelings of frustration for the bereaved, as they seem to be rejected if they cannot live up to the expectations of spectators who would like them to heal fast and return to 'normal functioning'. Self-care in terms of self-affirmation is important. Learning how to say "no" to unhelpful advices from friends who mean to be supportive is an essential tact.

Sandra wanted to take off her wedding ring in the memorial of Michael in front of all her friends and loved ones. She felt that she put on the wedding ring in front of loved ones and she should take it off now that the marriage had ended. Some of her friends reacted strongly to her decision and suggested to her that it could only be taken off one year later. Sandra felt she was being denounced and rejected by her friends, yet she also feared losing them and wanted to respect their feelings as well as her own. Finally she adapted her ritual of taking off the ring by putting her own ring, Michael's ring and her engagement ring onto a necklace so that the rings are always close to her heart.

12. CELEBRATE MARITAL LIFE NO MATTER HOW LONG

With the love for each other, set personal goals of living a rich and fulfilling life so that the spouse can die without regrets. Celebrate marital life no matter how long. Bereaved persons can establish personal growth and transformational goals after bereavement. Allow yourself to be happy and free. Do not lock oneself in the chains of grief, self-blame and regrets. Develop a checklist of inspirations from the past and move on with life.

Sandra visited friends in the Philippines and incidentally, on Michael's birthday, Sandra went to a town called St Michael. Sandra regarded this coincidence as a positive message that Michael was sending her: that he will always be around her.

13. REALIGNMENT OF LIFE PRIORITIES

Robert Neimeyer proposed the term of realigning life priorities after bereavement. This is an existential search for what is more important in the here and now. There are lots of uncertainties that bereaved persons, especially spouses, have to face after the death of a loved one.

> **Sandra:** I, you know, I don't know where it is going to take me in terms of my work, because there [are] new desires and impacts and things and directions in which I'm going that I am no longer fighting. I am scared. I'm scared that if I stop doing what I did then blah blah blah blah blah, but I'm holding that fear. Making the time for this interview, making the time for the counselling, not filling it with doing other things.
>
> And each day that I have, the hours that I have are so precious, that there's no room for things that aren't priorities still. So I really know where those priorities are, and I'm sifting out what isn't just critical, 'cause there isn't time, and there especially isn't time if I look after myself and give myself rest. there is no time. I only have what there is, and I don't know how much or little of that I will have, if I have till the next hour or till I'm 80.

14. APPRECIATE PERSONAL GROWTH AFTER BEREAVEMENT

It can be scary to have to confront new challenges of handling funeral arrangements, as well as tax, legal and insurance issues after the death of a loved one. It can be a steep learning curve and the transformation can be fast too.

> **Sandra:** I learn something new, yeap, so the financial, the legal... very slow. Changing over household bills, bank accounts all very slow, and I do, I just plough away, and a lot of big things hit, and then you kind of have to respond quickly. Tax, that was a huge big thing that hit me and we had to respond really fast, yet managed to pull that off with the very kind help of our new bookkeeper who a friend and colleague introduced us to at just the right time.

15. CONTINUING BOND

Complete loss of touch with a deceased spouse is among the many heartbreaking thoughts; trying to continue the legacy of the deceased may help to establish a continuing bond. Establish new personal goals in living a meaningful life, as it is a fulfilment of promise made to a spouse before his or her death.

Keeping books, clothes and furniture at home was a way to remember Michael. Although Sandra would have liked to redecorate her home, Diana refused to throw anything away because every piece of furniture belongs to Daddy. It was after long negotiations that a gradual plan of repainting the home was agreed upon. Similar stories of differences among family members on deciding what to keep and what to throw away were found in the play of *The Rabbit Hole*.

16. BEREAVEMENT CAN BE A LIFE-TRANSFORMING EXPERIENCE

Pain of bereavement may take months and years to slowly subside while releasing energy for constructive actions. The more attached the deceased and the bereaved are to each other, the harder it is for the latter to rebound.

However, by overcoming this existential crisis of spousal death, one can realign one's life priorities and clarify passions in life and related commitments. Chinese people believe in the statement: 'Bitterness is the best medicine.' Artists and poets are most creative during moments of grief and mourning. By focusing on the transformational growth and inspirations in life through grief, many bereaved spouses shared with us their journeys of surprises and new discoveries in life.

> **Sandra:** Gosh I actually think there's so many [lessons to learn], which is very interesting. This has been an experience unlike any other that has fundamentally changed me. Fundamentally, in terms of my own experience and knowledge and understanding of dying and all the things I learned from you and from my process of living with dying, that if I look at the growth out of that pain, that's incredible growth...

When Michael actually died by my side, and I have a photo of just after that moment and I have to look at that 'cause it's on my phone. So he's just died and I very much feel his presence with me and I look at his face and my face and there were times when he was dying that I wanted to die, or it felt like I was also dying, and yet we all sort of went through that process recognising that I wasn't dying, I was here making choices, I was still alive, and I was making choices to be alive.

One day it'll be my turn to die.[...]There is a real existential experience of truth from that which now impacts my whole life, in fact impacts every decision. It's that I find, I mean how invaluable it is. I am not going to go through my life ignoring that, however painful. And then if I think about just all the practical ways, that each day I have reached out to find ways, both through Michael's illness [and] since his dying, that takes a lot of skill. I feel proud of myself in that, I feel proud of myself as a mum, I feel proud of all these things I'm doing. I just get very scared.[...]

So that's powerful learning about the here and now, but I'm still learning in that as well, because knowing that truth is: (a) living with the pendulum emotional swing, (b) knowing that there is no certainty which a lot of people can happily pretend there is and I can't because I know there isn't. Sometimes that's just terrifying, sometimes that's exciting, and it also just, it is, a very powerful learning, and it's tricky then to sort of plan, you know, do I plan as if I have 80 years, plan as if I have an afternoon. And if I plan as if I have an afternoon then I'll go and spend all the money in my bank account, and if I plan until I am 80 then I've got all these other things in place and everything. Every plan, every decision becomes a real choice.

CONCLUSION: THERE IS NO SUFFERING THAT THE SOUL DOES NOT PROFIT FROM

Achieving a dignified death, enriching bereavement and fulfilling life are possible with adequate preparation for death. The stories of individuals clearly demonstrate that people can 'SET and Go' on with their life as dying patients and bereaved persons throughout the process of end-of-life, dying and bereavement. The pathways of grieving should also be measured in terms of growth, meaning-making, discovery and transformation, instead of only by depression.

Future researches on resilience and transformation through SET and Go would be worthy of investigation.

References

Bonanno, G.A., Wortman, C.B., Lehman, D.R., Tweed, R.G., Haring, M., Sonnega, J., Carr, D., & Nesse, R.M. (2002). 'Resilience to Loss and Chronic Grief: A Prospective Study from Preloss to 18-Months Postloss'. *Journal of Personality and Social Psychology, 83(5),* 1150–1164.

Byock, I.R. (1996) 'The Nature of Suffering and the Nature of Opportunity at the End of Life'. *Clinical Geriatric Medicine.* 12(2), 237–252.

Chan, C.L.W. & Chow, A.Y.M. (eds.) (2006). *Death, Dying and Bereavement— The Hong Kong Chinese Experience.* Hong Kong: Hong Kong University Press.

USA

Dr. Robert A. Neimeyer
Professor and Director of Psychotherapy Research, Department of Psychology,
University of Memphis
http://web.mac.com/neimeyer/Home/About_Me.html

UK

Dr. Terry Cooper
Founder Director of Spectrum
http://www.spectrumtherapy.co.uk

Dr. Charles Neal
Independent Psychotherapist, Supervisor and Consultant
http://www.charles-neal.com

HONG KONG

Dr. Cecilia Chan
Professor of the Department of Social Work and Social Administration,
University of Hong Kong
Author of In Celebration of Life: A Self-help Journey of Preparing for Death and
Living with Loss and Bereavement (published by the Centre on Behavioural Health,
University of Hong Kong, 2009)
http://cbh.hku.hk

Project Enable
A valuable source of support offered in Chinese and English. The Centre on
Behavioral Health at the University of Hong Kong runs the Empowerment Network
for Adjustment to Bereavement and Loss in End-of-life (ENABLE), a project funded
by the Hong Kong Jockey Club Charities Trust. It serves to educate the general
public on effective death preparation as well as to promote enhanced adjustment to
bereavement and loss.
http://www.enable.hk

Sandra Keys
Director of Caretta Limited
sandra.keys@caretta.com.hk

Acknowledgements

This book is a testament to the true value of friendship and to the power of a loving global community. Through my writing, I offer our family and friends a permanent, heart-felt legacy of gratitude. Good friends are not only fair-weather friends, they are the people who really stand by you when times get tough. We are truly blessed to have you in our lives. Please know that my words will never actually be enough to fully express how grateful I feel on behalf of me and my family.

We have also been privileged over these past years to lean on the kindness of strangers who have shown through their behaviour what it is to really care without expectation of anything in return. Our life path has brought us into contact with people of many different nationalities, religions and backgrounds from whom we have received nothing but care and support. In the light of this experience I cannot help but question why violence is so much more the norm in other parts of our society and to sincerely wish for change.

I would like to give special mention to those who have provided me with the professional support and training that has played such a formative role in my life and work to date.

Before we moved to Hong Kong as a family in November 1999, I trained for ten years at Spectrum, a centre for humanistic psychotherapy in North London in the UK. I also later also set up a professional practice there. Thank you Terry Cooper and Jenner Roth for founding Spectrum and for being such inspirational teachers in my life. Thank you also to Anna Patterson. My ten years of personal work with you set a strong foundation of learning in place from which I have been able to grow. To all the other staff members, colleagues and friends at Spectrum, I thank you for the important roles that you have played and will continue to play in my life.

Special thanks is given to Charles Neal. Charles you offered our family a bridge between London and Hong Kong when you first introduced us to your friends Debra Ziegler and Colin Lewin. None of us knew at the time just exactly how important this bridge would turn out to be. You have since walked by my side. You are the midwife who has guided me through the creation of this book and who then assisted final delivery with your detailed and sensitive editing. My love and sincere thanks go to you.

For my professional support in Hong Kong, my sincere thanks go to Neil Cowieson. Neil, you offered me my first job in Hong Kong eight years ago and I am very proud to still be working by your side today. You have been my boss, you are also my friend, colleague, mentor and coach. There have been times when I would not have been able to keep going without your support, when you literally picked up and held my business for me despite the pressures you were under at the time. Thank you. I would also like to give special mention to Vivian Leigh, Pennie Wong and Rachel Autherson for also working by my side in Hong Kong and for just taking work projects off my hands without questions at challenging times. My thanks also go to my clients for your care, concern and understanding over the years. I am very grateful to have been — and to continue to be — working with many of you over many years now.

In the final weeks leading up to Michael's death, my friend Sue was helping me to search for sources of support on the internet and she came across the work of Professor Cecilia Chan, Professor of the Department of Social Work and Social Administration. It has been my honour that Professor Chan (Ceci) walked by my side, supporting and guiding me through Michael's dying. Our counselling sessions together are now being shared with others through teaching films produced by the University of Hong Kong. One of my goals in writing this book is to be able to share the lessons that I learned from Ceci with others. In offering me practical tools as well as emotional support she helped me to turn a very painful experience into a transformational and meaningful one.

Through Ceci, I was introduced to Dr. Robert A. Neimeyer (Bob) when I attended a workshop that he was running here in Hong Kong. I consider it to be a great privilege to have had the opportunity to learn from two of the world's leading experts in death education and counselling. They have so much experience from which we can learn. My personal thanks to the university also go to Pandora Ng. Pandora, your supervision through the publication of my book has offered me invaluable support not least in managing the emotional impact of my work. And to Alicia Poon. Alicia, you are a wonderful child psychologist and I am so grateful to you for holding Diana's hand alongside me.

More thanks go to Peter Sherwood for allowing me to learn from you as a published author; to Martin Alexander for your support as a published poet in introducing me to Dania Shawwa Abuali at Haven Books just when my own emotional resources were at a low; to Dania for lending your wholehearted personal and professional support to getting my book into print; to Jilly Mangles for the hours that you spent as a friend on sensitively editing my final draft manuscript; to Edward Mangles for your inspiration on the title of my book and to Michelle Low for working with me on the final editing process.

Last, yet by no means least, my thanks to all those who have been open in sharing with me your own experiences of living with terminal illness and bereavement and the ways that you have learnt to cope with them. These ways include precious acts of creativity such as writing poetry dedicated to the tragic loss of a brother when he was very young. One of my main goals in writing this book is to encourage us all to be open in talking with and in learning from each other about subjects that are often seen as frightening and even taboo ones to avoid.

A Special Thank-You to Our Village Head
衷心感謝塘福村村長及當地居民於Michael追悼會上作出的配合，以及他們一直對我和家人寄予無限的支持與關懷。

About the Author

Sandra Keys was born Diana Freda Downes on 21st January 1964 and was handed over for adoption six weeks later, after which she was raised Sandra Margaret Entwistle. Sandra spent the first 17 years of her life growing up in Bolton, in the North of England, with her parents and her sister Alison, before moving to the University of Edinburgh, where she graduated with an MA in French and Business Studies. Her specialist subject was existential French literature. She then moved to live and work in and around London.

Sandra married Michael Keys in February 1993, and gave birth to their daughter, Diana, in January 1999. In November 1999, the family moved to Hong Kong and, less than two weeks later, Michael was diagnosed with a heart tumour that turned out to be a very rare form of heart cancer, cardiac leiomyosarcoma. Michael lived for eight years—rather than the predicted six months—following his original diagnosis, resulting in him being one of, if not the, world's longest living survivor of cardiac leiomyosarcoma.

Combining her interest in understanding people and existential issues with her training in business and love of travel, Sandra has successfully established a career in management and human resources development. Her work in the corporate world, in both the private and public sectors, now spans 20 years, the past ten of which have been spent in the Asia-Pacific region. She also has ten years of training in counselling and psychotherapy, with professional experience underpinned by ongoing personal development work at Spectrum in the UK.